Lots of luck

CHARLIE HUSTLE

CHARLIE HUSTLE

By Pete Rose with Bob Hertzel

An Associated Features Book

PRENTICE-HALL, INC., Englewood Cliffs, N.J.

10 9 8 7 6 5 4 3 2 1

Library of Congress Cataloging in Publication Data

Rose, Pete
  Charlie Hustle.

  "An Associated Features book."
  1. Rose, Pete 2. Baseball.
I. Hertzel, Bob, joint author. II. Title.
GV865.R65A295   796.357'092'4 [B]   75-5517
ISBN 0-13-448209-3

To all the good baseball fans everywhere

Introduction

It was six baseball seasons ago when I first walked into the locker room of the Cincinnati Reds and met Peter Edward Rose. By his measuring stick, that's 1,228 hits back, an average of 204 per season. I've seen them all as a reporter for the Cincinnati *Enquirer*. Pete Rose then was known as Charlie Hustle. He still is. It is a title he has earned as a player, a nickname of which he is justly proud.

In those six seasons, though, a tremendous change came over the man who is Charlie Hustle. It is something more than just a change in hair style. Once, of course, he was among the last of flat tops. Today he is mod from the top of his shag cut to the tip of his platform shoes.

But the change in Pete Rose has been an inner change, an alteration of the man himself. From a "hot dog" to a leader. And 1974 was a difficult year for many leaders. Pete Rose and the Cincinnati Reds battled for a pennant while the President of the United States resigned amid the Watergate scandal, and at times it seemed Rose was hardly more popular than Richard Nixon.

A year earlier, Rose fought Bud Harrelson in the dirt at Shea Stadium and the incident labeled Rose a bully in the eyes of many people. That is an image derived from Rose's consuming will to win. The public decided that Rose was a villain and throughout the 1974 season he was subjected to harassment that he neither deserved nor understood.

The man belies that image. But for a leader at the center of a storm, it isn't easy to sort out the two.

Out of all this emerged this book, a diary that brings out the frustrations suffered by a man who is in love with a game—a man who knows nothing but victory, yet has never won a world's championship.

I have lived on the road with Pete Rose and seen him operate. I have watched him play baseball with a dedication seldom seen in American life today. I have laughed with him through the moments of humor, enjoyed his victories, including three batting titles and a Most Valuable Player award, and suffered with his defeats.

This one year of Pete Rose's life was one that Pete Rose will never forget. I will not forget it either.

Bob Hertzel

CHARLIE HUSTLE

This was the night the city of New York was waiting for. It was the New York Baseball Writers' Dinner, an affair that was to bring together the likes of Mickey Mantle, Joe DiMaggio, Whitey Ford, and Willie Mays.

It was also to bring together Bud Harrelson and me. It was our first meeting since that day in October 1973 when we fought at second base in Shea Stadium in the third game of the playoffs—playoffs the Mets were to win while the fans worked me over.

I was attending the banquet at the Hotel Americana to receive the Good Guy Award from the New York writers. No joke. The real thing and it wasn't meant as a gag. They liked the way I handled myself in the midst of all that trouble with Harrelson and they liked the way I've always been honest and available to reporters. The joke part of it was that Harrelson was chosen to present the award to me. That was supposed to be funny but I figured I had to top even that.

So, as soon as I saw that little Met shortstop, I walked up, threw my arms around him, and planted a big kiss on his kisser. I think that got the point across. Certainly, it got some laughs. I mean, I'm not mad at Bud Harrelson and never have been.

I'm not going to apologize for all those goings-on during the 1973 playoffs. I'm not sorry about anything. I'm not sorry about the way it happened, my sliding hard into Harrelson in trying to break up a double play. I'm only sorry it didn't

1

inspire my team to the pennant won by the New York Mets two days later. The whole thing was baseball the way it's supposed to be played. I'm no damn little girl out there. I'm supposed to give the fans their money's worth and play hard and try to bust up double plays and shortstops. The free-for-all that followed is part of baseball.

It all happened on October 8 at Shea Stadium, fifth inning, the Mets leading, 9-2. I was on first with one out when Joe Morgan hit a ground ball behind me. I was running for second base when John Milner, the first baseman, caught the ball and threw to second. Now I didn't see whether he stepped on first. I didn't know if I was forced at second or if Harrelson had to tag me when the throw came. All I knew was that I had to go in hard. It turned out that Harrelson didn't have to tag me. He stepped on the base and threw to first to complete the double play. But I bounced up and hit Bud with an elbow, accidentally.

"You no-good punk," he shouted. "You hit me with an elbow."

"G'wan, get out of here," I said, thoroughly mad at the score and the double play. Next thing I knew, he was walking toward me. Now, I didn't want to fight. I could have decked him right there. I learned young that if you're going to fight, you throw the first punch. My dad, if he were still alive, probably would have given me hell for not unloading right away. But I wasn't mad at Bud and didn't want trouble. I didn't want him punching me, either. So I did what I thought was right. I grabbed him. He can't punch if I'm holding him.

Right about then I realized I was in the middle of the Met defense, right there at second base, and that trouble was starting. I figured I had to protect myself, so I threw Bud to the ground and pulled him over on top of me. Everything was lovely, I thought. Then I felt it. A shot in the back . . . a foot or a fist, I don't know. I know the replay showed Wayne Garrett there, and I guess it was him. Now the benches were

2

empty and the bullpens were rushing toward second base. Johnny Bench was there and he was pulling people off. Ted Kluszewski, maybe the strongest man in the world, had me and I knew I was in good hands. I couldn't move.

I figured it was over. Then, all of a sudden, it flared up again with Pedro Borbon, our relief pitcher, swinging at Buzz Capra, a Met reliever. They broke that up but Borbon, who is a wild man, was almost insensible with fury. He reached down, grabbed a cap, and put it on his head. It was Cleon Jones' Met cap.

"Pete," Borbon told me later, "I put that cap on and see blue all over my head. I grab it and I don't know what happen."

I had to laugh. I saw what he did. He took the cap off, tugged at it, stuck it in his mouth, bit it, tore it, and threw it away, piece by piece. All the while, Jones was walking behind him, trying to pick up the pieces of his cap.

The trouble didn't end with the fight. Now the fans—all 53,967 of them—were screaming for blood. They were throwing everything they could get their hands on. A whiskey bottle shot by my head. I was lucky; Gary Nolan, a pitcher who was on the disabled list, got hit on the side of the face with a half-full beer can.

That was it. Sparky Anderson, our manager, pulled the team off the field. They started making announcements to try to quiet the crowd. That just made them worse. Chub Feeney, the National League president, was running here and there and everywhere. Sparky wouldn't let us back on the field until there was order.

Finally a peace delegation was sent out to left field to negotiate a truce. The Mets sent Willie Mays, Tom Seaver, Cleon Jones, Rusty Staub, and Yogi Berra. I got a kick out of the way Red Smith, *The New York Times* sports columnist, described Berra the next morning. "A Henry Kissinger in knickers," was Smith's line.

3

They finally got some kind of peace restored, although everyone was worried—so worried that the umpires suggested I move to center field, out of harm's way. Imagine, here we are playing for the National League pennant and they want me out of position. They want to weaken the Cincinnati Reds because of the fans' behavior. "No way," I say.

We lost that game, and the next day I was on the spot. The fans were infuriated and displaying all kinds of obscene signs. We were down in the playoffs, 2-1, and had to win. But first the Mets wanted Harrelson and me to shake hands at home plate. No way. That would have been disaster. We're out there to win.

This game will forever stand out in my memory because I was playing against not only the Mets, but the whole city of New York. There were 53,000 fans booing me when I hit a twelfth-inning home run off Harry Parker to win the game.

Finally, it ended. We lost the playoffs, and the last game ended on a sour note. The Met fans went berserk. In the ninth inning the game had to be stopped twice.

Our owners were assaulted, driven out of their box seats by the crowd. Lois Ballou, wife of the team doctor, was knocked to the ground and trampled. Ann Buse had her hair pulled. They had to be rushed to safety.

And when the game ended, I was on base. The guys on the bench were fearing for my life. Johnny Bench had even suggested to Sparky that they send a pinch runner in for me.

I got to the dugout safely, running through the crowd that spilled onto the field. How worried were my teammates? Bench had them all armed with bats so they could fight their way out to rescue me if necessary.

And so it was that the season ended in violence and with Pete Rose being called a big bully. What did 1974 have in store for me?

Bob Howsam, president of the Cincinnati Reds, sat across from me, his large desk separating the two of us. "I never thought I'd be sitting here offering a man $150,000 to play baseball for me," he said.

I knew that Johnny Bench had walked in and told Mr. Howsam to fill in a figure and he'd sign the contract. Just like that. The figure Howsam filled in was enough, so Johnny jumped at it.

Not me, though. I wasn't settling for any $150,000. I wanted and I got a contract that called for $160,000. Not at all bad for a tough kid from the Western Hills area of Cincinnati.

I like Bob Howsam, even though I've had my difficulties with him over the years. A couple of times I had to hold out to get what I was worth. I didn't like it and he didn't like it, but in baseball you've got to make it when you can. You never know what's around the corner.

I remember in 1972 sitting in the office of Chief Bender, our director of player personnel, and having him tell me how important it was for me to sign the contract he was offering so that I, the team captain, could be the first Red to sign for the coming season. I had to laugh. A month or so earlier Gary Nolan had told me he had signed his contract.

The year that was worst of all, though, was 1971. The year before that I hit .316, scored 120 runs, got 205 hits and hit 15 homers. We broke all attendance records in Cincinnati and had become the Big Red Machine—a name I stuck on the team—while winning a pennant.

I figured I was due a big raise. Silly me. They told me I had "an off year" after winning consecutive batting titles. I couldn't believe it. They said I had "reached a plateau" in

5

salary and didn't figure to get much more than the $100,000 I was making. The offer called for no raise, and the Reds were in no mood to budge. Neither was I. I wasn't going to take that offer. I deserved a raise.

I held out, and let me tell you, things got pretty bitter. At one point I set up a conference call from Cincinnati with the club, myself, and my business advisor, Hy Ullner.

Hy wasn't going to take part in the negotiations. He wasn't acting as an agent. He was just going to listen and advise me. I set the call up at my expense. I put it through. I told them Hy was on the line.

No dice. They wouldn't talk to me with Hy listening. If he wanted to take part, they said, the only way it could be done was face to face in Florida. I had to tell Hy to hang up and cancelled the call.

As it turned out I got myself that raise. It wound up being something like $2,500. They decided to give me a cost-of-living raise, based on what an average player makes in the big leagues. For $2,500 they let me sit out two weeks of spring training. I felt I had won, at least in principle. I still wonder what some other player might have gotten walking in with the same statistics I had on a pennant-winning team.

That's in the past. Today I'm a Bob Howsam man. What a president he has made for the Reds! In 1973 we drew more than two million fans and that may be the most impressive statistic in baseball history. Cincinnati isn't exactly what you'd call a major metropolis.

Howsam first is a Cincinnati Reds man. He's working for baseball, too. He loves the game and worries about it going down in popularity.

One of the things he worries about is high salaries. He doesn't worry about it enough to keep Johnny Bench, Joe Morgan, Tony Perez, and me from getting six figures each. But he does think this trend may kill the game.

Howsam brought up the idea of high salaries killing the

6

game while we spoke. "I gave you a chance to end mine last year when I asked for a three-year contract," I told him. "I sat right here and asked you for a three-year contract and you didn't like the idea. It cost you $40,000."

Actually, it cost him $44,500 because that's the raise I got. Howsam doesn't believe in multi-year contracts. He says they're one-way streets. If a player has a good year, he wants to renegotiate. If he has a bad year, you don't see him.

I always speak straight to Mr. Howsam. We have that kind of relationship. It developed in 1973 when he finally realized that I am a man who can lead and started to take advantage of my leadership.

Sometimes when the team was on the road, he'd invite me up to his hotel room for breakfast. We'd sit there and talk about the team and what I could do to help Sparky.

Danny Driessen, our rookie third baseman, was one of the guys whose name came up during these discussions. Howsam wanted me to make sure he stayed straight.

Danny's name even came up during our contract talks. Seems he was unhappy with his contract offer and hung up on Chief Bender. The last guy to do that was Bobby Tolan and that came in the middle of his troubles with the club late in 1973. Tolan wound up being traded to San Diego.

Mr. Howsam likes Driessen and likes, especially, the way he hits. He wants to make sure Danny doesn't develop into a troublemaker.

February 28
Tampa

I picked up the newspapers this morning and saw it right there in the headlines: "ROSE SIGNS FOR $158,000." That's what it said. I could hardly wait to get to the ball park.

7

"Damn," I said when Jim Selman of the Tampa *Tribune* walked up. "You giving me a pay cut already?"

Jim had to laugh when I told him his figure was low. I've known him a long time. He was here back in the old days and we started talking about it. I played in Tampa my second year in pro ball and set one of the records I'm really proud of. I hit 30 triples that season. That's right, 30 triples. Plus I had two inside-the-park home runs and two more triples in the playoffs.

"How can you, just a day after signing a contract for $160,000, remember what happened back then?" Selman asked me.

"Easy. How can anyone forget making $400 a month and owning two pair of pants and three pair of socks? That's how I remember it," I answered.

Those were good days. I remember we won the Florida State League championship and our owner decided to give us something to remember that occasion with. He gave each one of us a Zippo cigarette lighter. Wonderful. I didn't even smoke.

We were standing around waiting for the workout to begin, the first workout of the spring, when Johnny Bench came up.

"Here," he said, throwing his arm around me, "is $312,000 worth of talent."

Larry Stahl, a reserve outfielder, heard Bench. He walked up, threw his arm around me from the other side, and said: "Now there's $322,000 worth of talent here."

That's how it goes with the Reds. Lots of laughs. Stars and reserves mixing it up, joking.

The Reds are a big, happy ship. That's one of the reasons I never thought about going to outside arbitration with my contract. This, of course, was the first year we could do that if we couldn't reach an agreement with the company.

It's one of the many benefits Marvin Miller has gotten through for us as "the players' commissioner."

I didn't like the idea of arbitration for me because I thought it might hurt the team. But for many players, it's a good idea and a necessary one.

Take Don Gullett, our young pitcher. He's a quiet kid who just doesn't like to sit there in an office and argue salary. He went out and got himself an agent, Jerry Kapstein. The result was a good raise. Alone and without the threat of arbitration, he would have signed for less.

And Tony Perez. He also employed Kapstein. He threatened to go to arbitration. He got a six-figure contract. Latin American players need protection. They have a language problem which doesn't help when they're negotiating.

We started our exercises and, let me tell you, they aren't easy. Some clubs work an hour and a half and go home. The Cincinnati Reds work an hour and a half and then get down to practicing.

I told Sparky he was "The Exercist."

"What?" he said.

"You work the devil out of us," I answered. He liked that.

The legs that I thought were in shape quickly get stiff and sore and I start thinking, "I must be getting old."

It isn't long, though, before it's time for fun and games. We start hitting. This is what I live for, and before the day's over, my hands will be raw with blisters. I love that kind of pain.

March 2
Tampa

"Damn," I shouted at the top of my lungs. I hopped out of the batting cage, the pain shooting up my leg.

9

Dick Baney, a right-hander, had been pitching batting practice. He threw one inside and I swung. The ball left the bat and traveled directly toward my right shin, hitting with all the impact of a sledgehammer.

Over to the screen I hobbled, the pain quickly going away.

"Damn, it's swollen already," I said. "And man, it's starting to hurt again."

A fan, looking through the screen, shouted, "Put some ice on it." That was just what I needed.

"Oh," I said, looking at him. "Is that what you're supposed to do? How about if I just rub dirt on it?" I was being sarcastic, but he didn't understand.

"That's okay if it's wet mud," the doctor in the house answered. I limped to the clubhouse and followed my "doctor's" orders. Ice was applied and I was through for the day.

Irony. I guess that's what it was. Not five minutes before I busted up my leg, I was standing by the cage with Sparky Anderson. Dave Concepcion was taking ground balls at shortstop. He was coming off a broken ankle. His running mate at second base, Joe Morgan, was coming off surgery to remove some calcium from his heel.

"We've got a shortstop with a bum ankle and a second baseman with a bum heel," I said to Sparky. "We'll be the only team in baseball that works on its double play in the whirlpool."

Now you can make room in the whirlpool for the lead-off man, too.

March 3
Tampa

Tony Perez sticks his head in my door at King Arthur's Inn.
"I ready for spring training now," he says.

10

He shows me a case of J & B.
Even ballplayers have to relax sometime.

I'm sitting in a bar with a reporter and photographer and talking to the bartender when this guy comes up to say hello. I get that all the time and I don't pay a whole lot of attention to the guy. Then, all at once, a bell goes off in my head.

"Tommy, what's happening?" I say. I recognize him. When I was a kid playing in Tampa, Tommy was tending bar over at the Hillsborough Hotel. "Where you been?" I ask Tommy.

"Been in jail. Five years ago I got busted and was run out of town by the prostitutes. They thought I ratted on them."

There were good times in the old days, I tell Tommy. He asks me about my running mates in those days, Tommy Helms and Art Shamsky. The memories start coming back.

"Remember when we stayed at the Hillsborough?" I say. "Me and Shamsky were coming back after curfew. We get to the hotel and can't go through the lobby because Phil Seghi, the farm director, is sitting there, so we decide to go up the fire escape.

"I guess someone heard us, though, and got scared. Called the house dick. Next thing I know there's a light shining at us and this guy is yelling, 'Stop or I'll shoot.' We stopped.

"What does the guy do? He brings us to Seghi. Seghi says, 'I know you weren't stealing. If I thought you were trying to shoot beavers I'd have you thrown out of baseball. Now, get to bed.' I was goddamn scared."

"You haven't changed, Pete," Tommy says.

11

I'm out doing my exercises and bitching. "Oakland doesn't do this," I shout and Larry Shepard, our pitching coach, hears me and comes up. He starts to tell me about what a wonderful thing it is to be doing your exercises. "Hell, the A's don't do it," I repeat. "It sure don't keep them from winning. All they have is $20,000 worth of championship rings on their fingers."

The pace changes. We go into one of those exercises designed to give you a breather—a little stretching of the leg muscles and about as much effort exerted as it takes to get out of bed in the morning.

"This is really doing a lot of good," I continue. "Why the hell do we have to do this?"

"You think you're tired?" Johnny Bench shouts. "You ought to follow me around all day. Catch batting practice. Run. Exercise. Warm up pitchers. You follow me and you'll really be tired."

"The only way you could tire me out would be if I followed you at night," I answer.

It isn't all bitching. Clay Carroll is doing his work next to me and when he's around you've just got to laugh. Carroll's nickname is Hawk and one look at his face is enough to tell you why.

An intellect Clay Carroll isn't. He's just a guy from off the farm down in Clanton, Alabama, who happens to be blessed with an arm that has an IQ of 160.

A couple of years back Carroll went out and bought himself a Lincoln Continental. He bought it from Bench and me when we had our car dealership. We gave him a helluva deal on an $8,000 car.

The damn car had everything, or so Hawk thought. That

12

was until the guys told him it had a built-in vacuum cleaner. He spent a month trying to find it. Never could. No wonder. There wasn't any.

"Clay Carroll buying a Continental is like putting earrings on a hog," my old roommate Tommy Helms said when Clay bought his car.

Tommy was always getting on Clay. I remember back in 1970, right after we moved into Riverfront Stadium. Of all people, it was Helms who hit the first Cincinnati home run in the park.

It wasn't exactly a memorable shot, a line drive that hit the foul screen about a foot above the left-field wall. The next day, though, Hawk and Wayne Granger, who was pitching for the Reds then, decided to mark the historic spot. They sneaked out and with adhesive tape put a big X on the spot where the baseball hit.

Helms walked out, saw the marking, and immediately said, "I know who did that. Had to be Hawk. He left his signature."

March 6
Tampa

When we're at spring training we stay at King Arthur's Inn. We've been there for ten years, starting back when it was called the Congress Inn. It's a nice place, not particularly fancy. We have two adjoining rooms, the main one having a kitchenette. I bring down my wife Karolyn, my two children, Pete, 4, and Fawn, 10, and my mother-in-law, who probably enjoys it more than any of us.

After practice today, I was out front playing with Googie, which is what I call my son Pete, and don't ask me why.

13

He is what you'd call a chip off the old block. All he wants to do is hit. You can't get him out in the field. But give him a bat and he's happy.

Now I don't believe in pushing him into baseball. He'll be able to do whatever he wants. But I have introduced him to it and he loves it.

Anyway, on this day I'm pitching to him and he's hitting line drive after line drive. He knows how to hit better than any 4-year-old I've ever seen.

Joe Bowen is a scout for the Reds and he checked into the hotel today. I was pitching and Pete was hitting and Joe stopped to look.

"Damn," he said, "who is that kid? He's got the best swing I've ever seen."

Pardon me if I have some fatherly pride. It must be the same feeling my father had with me.

I've got Googie hitting left-handed, even though he's a natural right-hander. I figure he'll be easy to change later when he should become a switch-hitter. And let me tell you, being a switch-hitter is an advantage. I can never thank my father enough for making me one when I was just a kid. I guess the year was 1950. I was 9 years old and trying out for my first organized team.

"Now you might run into a championship game, facing a right-handed pitcher," my father said to the manager. "But I want Pete to bat left-handed against every right-hander, no matter what. I want you to promise me that you'll let him switch hit."

That's how I became a switch-hitter. Just like that. I've been at it ever since, and now my goal is to become the greatest switch-hitter the game has ever known.

In 1973 I set a record for the most singles by a switch-hitter with 181. I want to own the record for most hits in a career by a switch-hitter, which Frankie Frisch now has at 2,880.

14

Spring training is a lot of things to a lot of different people. Me? I concentrate on working . . . hard. I like to go home at the end of the day tired, my hands hurting from hitting, my legs sore. Then I know I haven't been letting myself down.

My wife and kids swim and sometimes come out to watch the games. Little Googie really likes that.

The work is hard, sure, but it's supposed to be. You are getting ready for a grueling season of 162 games. To go through at top speed, as I do, you have to be in shape.

For relaxation, I sneak away to the track. I prefer the thoroughbreds at Florida Downs. After the workout, we'll pile three or four guys in a car and go over there.

At night, if I feel up to it, I'll take in the dogs or the jai alai. The big trouble with it all is that people never leave you alone. Take tonight. I went to the dog track.

Now when I handicap I look for speed and usually can find it. I can come up with a dog that is going for the front. Through five races, though, I haven't had a dog on top. In fact, I haven't had a dog any closer to the lead than fourth. Now I'm trying to handicap another race and, quite naturally, a guy comes up. "Hey, you're Pete Rose, aren't you?" the guy says.

"Yeah," I answer.

"Man, I love to see you do those head-first slides. How do you do that anyway?"

"You want me to show you here, on the concrete?"

"Naw. Hey, will you sign my program?"

So I sign and before you know it, other people are noticing me and I can't handicap the race. Funny, it doesn't bother me unless I'm losing.

Other guys have ways of killing time at spring training.

Most everyone brings his family down and they'll get together and party.

Golf, of course, is one of the more popular ways to spend an afternoon. Bench is on the course almost every day. He says he's mostly 280 to 300 yards off the tee. I'd love to get my game to the point where I could play with Johnny and take a few bucks from him, but I just don't have the patience to play golf. It isn't like tennis—quick, a lot of action.

Bench even runs a tournament for charity down here, but because I don't play golf, I don't go. I did have one good moment on a golf course. It came just before spring training in "The Superstars," which you might have seen on television. Kyle Rote, Jr., won the whole thing, but he didn't do anything in the running events. He didn't run the 100 and ran dead last in the half mile.

Anyway, my moment of glory on the golf course came when I was going against John Havlicek of the Boston Celtics. They tell me he normally shoots in the 80's, but on this day he was having nothing but trouble.

After eight holes John has a 54 and I have a 55. I actually haven't hit a good shot all day. On one hole I drove into the water and the ball skipped on top, hit the bank on the other side, and rolled onto the fairway.

So now we're walking to the final tee and I'm a shot behind. Havlicek takes an iron to make sure he doesn't hit the ball out of bounds. We are playing for fourth place in the tournament and it's worth a couple of hundred dollars.

Iron or no iron, he hits out of bounds. Then he tees off again and gets off a terrible drive.

I step up and split the fairway. Havlicek had missed the green. I make it. Havlicek three-putts finally; I get down in two and I beat him by two strokes.

"The Superstars" was fun. That O.J. Simpson was about

the greatest guy I've ever met. It's no wonder those guys at Buffalo knock themselves out blocking for him.

The first event down there was tennis and I drew the skier Karl Schranz. No one gave me a chance. He was supposed to be the best in the bunch and I had been playing just three months.

But they didn't count on my determination. He had me five games to two when I made a diving return to save the game. I mean, it was some kind of shot. So good that I broke the crystal in my Mickey Mouse watch. I went on to win that in overtime.

The next player I drew was Jim McMillian, the Buffalo Braves' basketball player.

I had him 5-2 and game point when I blew an easy shot. He came back to beat me and went on to the finals, losing to Rote.

Weight lifting. I'd never done that before. I didn't even know how to do it. And, I'll tell you, Bob Howsam was worried about it.

He called me, asked me to withdraw and, when I wouldn't, he begged me to have someone show me what I was doing. He didn't want me pulling anything.

Well, I did better weight lifting than I would have done swimming. I swam in the qualifying round and it was about the worst feeling I've ever had. By the time I finished, everyone already was out of the pool.

When I got out, the world was spinning like I'd just overdone it at a New Year's Eve party.

March 9
Bradenton

Danny Driessen had two hits today as we beat the Pirates,

4-2. That is not unusual. It seems Danny Driessen has two hits every day. He may just be the best young hitter in baseball today. He reminds me of myself. You can't defense him. He hits out of a deep crouch and sprays the ball over creation.

Last year he was hitting .409 at Indianapolis when we called him up. He hit .301 the rest of the way for us. Not bad for a kid who came out of nowhere.

"What'd you get to sign?" I asked him today.

"They gave me a yearbook and plane ticket," he laughed. "And I missed the plane. I had to take a bus to my first spring training."

That's just about how it went with him, too. The scouts somehow missed Danny Driessen. He went through the free-agent draft without being claimed. The reason was that he never played high school baseball. Oh, he tried to get a team started in high school. He went to the principal about it; the principal told him and his friends to go to the auditorium and wait for him.

"He never showed," Danny said. "I took the hint."

To this day, Danny swears that his older brother Bill was the better ballplayer, and he may be right, if you can believe the letter that got the Reds interested.

Harold Young was a schoolteacher in Hardeeville, North Carolina, 30 miles from Hilton Head, which is Driessen's home town. With no high school team, Danny played on Young's Sunday team. Young would drive the 30 miles over to pick up the two Driessens, then take them back home after the game.

Finally, he sat down and wrote the Reds a letter, describing Bill as 6-foot-3, 215 pounds with a 34-inch waist.

"Bill hits the ball regularly well beyond 425 feet on both his right and left sides [a switch-hitter with power, wow]. I am sure that he can throw the ball on a line to home plate from a distance of 375 feet in the outfield.

18

"If you put him on the mound, you would have the strength of Bob Gibson or Sandy Koufax. We do not use Bill on the mound because we do not have fellows to catch him. He wears out two or three catchers (swollen hands)."

And the letter also mentioned 17-year-old Danny, who was a catcher and outfielder, but a better catcher. The Reds got the letter, held a tryout for Driessen and signed him for a yearbook and a plane ticket. Might be the best investment they ever made.

I feel a little sorry for the kid, though. He's always been a first baseman and they are making him into a third baseman, and he just can't handle it yet. He's going to cost us some games over there, but his bat should more than make up for it.

March 12
Tampa

I was standing out near home plate the other day when we played the Pirates. Danny Murtaugh, the Pittsburgh manager, was chewing away on his wad of tobacco. A girl writer, Susan Lennis from Indianapolis, walked up to talk to him and you should have seen the show he put on. He spit that tobacco juice right between her feet, not getting a drop on her.

I call that accuracy.

Chewing tobacco is almost a lost art today. You can't find anyone outside of the mountains or the big leagues who does it.

I don't chew. Never could get the hang of it. But we have a few guys on the team who do. I guess they got started back when Ted Uhlaender came to us from the Cleveland Indians.

Now there was a guy who loved his chaw. He even

19

chewed in the hotel room at night. He roomed with Joe Hague and Hague swears that Uhlaender would have a plug in his cheek when he went to bed. When Uhlaender showed up, we were hooked on bubble gum and sunflower seeds. Pretty soon, though, we had us some real chewers. Alex Grammas is probably the coolest. He doesn't seem to ever spit. He just chews away and I'll be damned if I know what he does with the juice.

Then there's Bench. He never could get hooked on the bubble gum. It would always stick to his mask and that could be very distracting. Watch him sometime when he's catching. He's always flipping the mask up. I thought it was for the photographers, but he swears it's so he can spit.

Andy Kosco is another guy who chews, but he has one major problem. He can't hit with a wad in his mouth. So, every time Sparky tells him he's going to pinch-hit, this big wad of tobacco comes flying out of our dugout. It's like a sign that the other team steals. They know who the hitter is going to be.

Grammas, who has been around forever, says Bill Mazeroski, the old second baseman, is the best chewer he's ever seen. Nellie Fox and Pedro Ramos always had a big chew sticking out, stretching their cheek. And Harvey Kuenn, an American League batting king, wouldn't be caught without one.

They tell me that Rocky Bridges could actually knock a bug out of the air.

Finally, I guess, comes Don Lock of the Philadelphia Phillies. He was a right-handed hitter and a left-handed chewer. One day he went to the plate and got beaned. Took one square in the left jaw. The doctors said later the tobacco was all that saved him from serious injury.

Who says tobacco can be harmful to your health?

I haven't been getting enough batting practice lately. I figure I'd better take some extra hitting so I run over to the minor league camp.

A bunch of young kids are hitting. I jump in right after this big kid. He looks like a pretty good hitter to me. But, like most big, young kids, he has his problems.

"You're trying to pull everything," I say to him. "Watch this."

I hit a line drive to left. One to center. Another to left.

"It's all in the hands. This is the way to do it. You use your arms."

I'm just trying to help, but he's not paying any attention to me.

All the while I'm hitting and talking and teaching. And a crowd of minor league players is gathering. They're listening to every word. But not the guy I started with.

Finally, he turns to one of the guys who has come over to get this free lesson in hitting.

"Who is that guy?" he asks the kid next to him.

"That's Pete Rose," answers the other player.

All of a sudden, this big kid is very attentive. He's asking questions.

That made me feel good. I feel I may have helped this kid some as he tries to make it to the big leagues, as I did, and I feel I might have helped the Cincinnati Reds some.

Gary Nolan hasn't thrown a baseball hard all spring and that's a damn shame. When he's healthy, he's as good a pitcher as there is in the National League . . . in fact, in baseball.

He had twelve games of minor league experience when he came to the big leagues, won a spot on our staff during spring training, and went on to 14-8 with 2.58 earned-run average.

Not bad for a 19-year-old kid. Nolan could throw hard in those days, really hard. But he had a funny motion and hurt his arm.

I remember that first year Nolan was with us and eating up the league. Larry Jansen, then the Giants' pitching coach, noticed the motion. "He'll never last. He's got to hurt his arm," said Jansen.

Sure enough, the next season there was arm trouble. Again in 1969 the arm went bad. He no longer could throw a baseball through a car wash without getting it wet, but because of the bum arm he learned how to pitch.

Nolan came up with the best change-up in baseball and fought his way back to the big leagues, winning 18 and losing 7 in 1970 to help us to the pennant. Of course, his arm was hurting at the end of the season.

In 1972 you had to see Gary to believe him. At the All-Star break he had 13-2 but the arm was going fast. He finished the season nursing his shoulder but with a 15-5 record and 1.99 earned-run average.

The 1973 season was a big zero and you've never seen anyone more discouraged than Nolan. They tried everything: injections, pills, heat, exercise. They even thought they had it cured when they pulled an abscessed tooth.

This past winter, after he pitched all of two times in 1973, they tried killing a nerve in his arm with an electrified needle.

All that's left is surgery and that's what they're thinking about. That or releasing Gary. Actually, surgery is almost an impossibility because it would mean he would miss another year of pitching and his arm just couldn't take that.

So here we were, him with a bum wing and me with my bum wheel, staying behind while the team was playing the Braves in West Palm.

Gary came up to me and let me get just a brief look inside him.

"Pete, I've been dead a year and a half and they haven't even given me a funeral," he said.

Tragic. And, he's only 25.

March 19
Tampa

This is the day everyone has been waiting for. This afternoon in St. Petersburg it will be the Cincinnati Reds against the New York Mets for the first time since last October. World War III revisited. Tom Seaver will be pitching for the Mets.

But this one is going to have to go on without me. I'm not gonna play.

One of the reasons is the leg. It's still hurting and swollen. Another reason is my batting stroke. I want to work on that some.

And, of course, there's another reason. We play the Mets again Sunday and that one's on television back home. I want to do it on television. It will be more fun that way.

Funny, I'm not all juiced up thinking about playing the Mets. Harrelson and I are friends again. Of course, I still carry a bitch about Wayne Garrett. He hit me in the back, and sometime this year I'm going to get even.

It'll be clean, but I'll get him. Right now I'm just hoping that sometime I'm on first when Morgan singles to right. I hope it's close because I'm going into third head first but a little late. I'll leave him in the dugout.

23

I am no longer 0-for-March. We played the Dodgers today and I got my first three hits of the spring. That made me a whole lot happier than the final score, which showed the Dodgers winning, 5-3.

I could be much happier about my performance, too. I'm pulling the ball too much. All three hits were pulled. When I'm hitting well, I'm hitting the ball all over.

Something else made me mad. I should have had four hits. I don't like losing hits I should have, even in spring training.

I hit a bullet back through the middle. It caught Charley Hough, the Dodger knuckle-baller, right on the knee and bounced off. I hit it so hard that Dave Lopes, the second baseman, hadn't had time to react, so he was in position to field the ball and throw me out.

I'm still not too thrilled about what I've been seeing with the Reds. It's about time Sparky held a team meeting, something he does about as often as the Reds win a World Series. He doesn't believe in them.

The winning attitude isn't there yet and we're doing just about everything wrong that can be done. Hal King couldn't catch cold behind the plate today. Merv Rettenmund and Ken Griffey let a fly ball fall between them. No one called the damn ball.

Merv is new to center field, and I pulled him off to one side and told him that he has to remember to call everything because he's a center fielder now.

That's especially true with Griffey, who still is just a kid and who lacks major league experience. He has raw talent but he's going to have to work.

Like today. He was on first base when Dave Concepcion hit a pop-up ten stories high. Griffey was running on the pitch and never looked back. He went to second, stood there, finally saw the ball and couldn't get back to first. He was doubled off.

March 21
Tampa

George Zuraw scouts for the Reds and he's a helluva guy—the kind of guy you like to sit and talk to. He knows ballplayers and can spot one where no one else does.

One player he spotted a few years back was a kid named Rose. He was scouting for Pittsburgh then and they asked him if he would recommend trading Willie Stargell even up for Pete Rose.

Both of us were in the minor leagues then, Stargell at Asheville, North Carolina, in the Sally League and me in the Florida State League at Tampa. Stargell was looking like a star and I looked like a skinny kid who could do nothing but hustle.

Fact is the year before that Phil Seghi, then our farm director, got one report on me. It said I couldn't hit, run, throw, or field.

"All Rose can do is hustle," the report said.

Zuraw saw something more. "I turned in the longest report I'd ever turned in on a player and you were the subject," he told me. "I said you'd make a lot of money in baseball and you'd make a lot of money for baseball. I could see you'd bring people to the park."

Words like that make you feel good. Also maybe a little old. Especially when I think back to the way I signed my first contract with the Reds. I was what you might call a risk.

I had attended Western Hills High in Cincinnati. Most guys go through high school in four years. It took me five. I played every kind of sport possible in high school.

After flunking my sophomore year—I found more

25

interesting things to do that year than go to school—I wound up playing two years of varsity football and baseball.

In fact, the last year I played football was the last year Western Hills beat our archrival, Elder High. We won, 31-14, and I scored a touchdown, kicked an extra point, and ran another.

I was a skinny kid back in those days and I probably never would have signed if it weren't for my uncle, Buddy Bloebaum, who was a scout.

He arranged things with the Reds. We went to Crosley Field and my uncle talked to Phil Seghi. They gave me $7,000 and set it up so that I got another $5,000 if I went on a major league roster and lasted 30 days.

March 22
Tampa

A guy like me, who goes and goes and goes, enjoys his sleep almost as much as he enjoys a game-winning single off Bob Gibson. And man, I was enjoying my sleep. I'd finished playing nine innings against the Phillies, picking up a double off Steve Carlton and a walk.

Right there, in the middle of this beautiful dream, the phone rings. I reach over, pick it up and say something clever like "Huh?"

"Pete, did I wake you?"

"No," I answer, "I had to get up to answer the phone."

"Really, this is important. They've got me in the can."

It's a buddy from Cincinnati. Not a real close friend, but a guy I know who's staying at King Arthur's Inn, too.

"They got me on drunk driving," he says.

"What's that got to do with me?" I answer.

"Well, the bond's $500 and I don't have any money with

26

me. But I've got $500 in my room. They won't let me come get it. Think you could get it for me?"

"Yeah," I answer.

I roll out of bed, toss on some clothes, and call Buddy, the bellman. We go together over the guy's room and find his money. I figure I'd better go with Buddy to make sure the guy doesn't accuse him of stealing any.

Good thing, too. There isn't $500 there. Only $420.

Buddy brings it down to the city jail. Not enough. My late-night pal spends the night in jail until he can come up with the other $80.

It took me a while to get back to sleep and man, I was tired today. But I got a break. It rained and we didn't play.

Maybe it wasn't a break. Went to the racetrack at Florida Downs. That's an expensive way to spend an off-day.

March 23
Tampa

I became, of all things, a newspaperman today. A real journalist.

It all started when I came back from the ball park, my tail dragging. Two guys were there with my wife, doing an interview. Karolyn has made herself into quite a celebrity, doing her own radio show and the like. They even want her to make speeches.

These two kids—Pete Alexis and Dennis Greulle—are from a new sports weekly paper in Cincinnati that's going to be called *The Reds Alert*.

I remember the kids. Back in January they contacted Ann Smith, who works as my agent. They asked her if I'd be interested in lending my name to the paper and doing a column. She said we certainly were.

27

So they started negotiating. They were from Minnesota but they'd come to town and talk. First thing you know we were ready to go to spring training and they couldn't get together with Ann.

Ann's always reaching for the moon. She always wants front money and they couldn't come to an agreement.

So now I recognize the kids.

"I thought you were the guys I'm supposed to be in the newspaper business with," I say, and they say yeah, but they couldn't get together with Ann. She was asking for financial statements and things like that.

"Goddamn," I said. "I'm not signed exclusively with Ann. You guys should have come to me. I'd be happy to talk with you."

So, we talked. I mean these two kids, early 20's, were optimistic as hell. They wanted to do it with pictures, interviews, offbeat stuff.

"Look, get some kind of contract together and talk to me," I said.

The next day I met with them and Bill Matthews, president of Landmark Community Newspapers, and I decided to sign with them. No front money. I'm going to be the good guy, do a column, all that jive and get nothing up front. It's settled.

March 25
Tampa

Today I find out that they offered Ann five grand up front. I mean I'm mad. I'm trying to help and they screw me out of five grand.

"How come you guys offer Ann $5,000 front money and you talk to me and won't give me any front money?" I say.

28

"We decided we just didn't have the front money," they say.

Now I call Ann. I tell her about it.

"Look, I know I signed the damn thing, but see if you can't call Bill Matthews and renegotiate. Get the front money," I say.

She got it all. The front money. Twenty percent of advertising. A dollar per subscription. A newspaper empire is born.

All I do is give them a column a week. I pick out which one of the guys goes on the cover and which one of the wives will be interviewed.

"Look," Pete Alexis says, "what if the newspaper wants to take a stand that's anti-Reds?"

"Okay with me, as long as you make it plain that I'm only responsible for my column."

March 26
Orlando

I almost killed someone today. I mean I had the bottom of my stomach just drop out and my heart sink. For one fleeting instant I thought I'd killed Joe Decker, who is a good, young pitcher for the Minnesota Twins.

There was one out when I came to the plate in the top of the third. I hit one back through the middle, a vicious line drive. In fact, I can't hit a baseball any harder than I hit that one.

Decker barely saw it coming. It lashed into his head and bounced all the way back to the Minnesota dugout. He went down as though he was hit by a bullet.

I've hit pitchers before with line drives, but never with one like that. A couple of inches lower, he would have been hit in the temple and might have been killed.

I ran to first, then went over to see how he was. He was still conscious, but he wasn't at all sure what had happened.

"I thought I'd gotten it in the face for sure, but I guess I had my head turned just enough," Decker said later.

Just enough. Good thing. It's amazing, though, that only one man in all of baseball history has ever been killed. A pitcher stands just 60 feet, 6 inches from home plate and is about 54 feet away when he finally releases the ball.

With all the line drives back through the middle, it's only a matter of time until someone gets seriously injured or killed. Take Herb Score. He damn near lost an eye, and had his career ruined when Gil McDougald of the New York Yankees got him.

I wish there was something they could do about it, but there isn't. Maybe they could move the rubber back a couple of feet, ha, ha.

March 27
Lakeland

Bumpity-bump goes the bus. Just like the old days in the Florida State League, off from Tampa for Lakeland. A night game against the Detroit Tigers.

I'm up at the front of the bus as I usually am, and I see Andy Kosco sitting off to one side. He looks serious. Must not be hitting too well.

Andy originally signed with the Tigers. They thought he was going to be another Al Kaline, and gave him a whole bunch of money. Sixteen cities and fourteen years later, here he is, a reserve with the Cincinnati Reds riding a bus to play against Detroit.

Kosco's the nicest guy you'd ever want to meet. Never has a bad word for anyone. And hard-working, man. He's been going to college during the off-season for eleven years at Youngstown State University trying to get a law degree. "If I had it to do over again, I'd get the college out of the way before I signed," he told me.

He's the same way with baseball. Built himself a batting cage at home. It has a pitching machine and everything. I guess during the winter when he's not hitting the books, he's hitting baseballs.

I asked him about it after we recalled him from Indianapolis. "I'm not a super player and I realize that," he told me. "I need all the advantages I can get. I try to get as much hitting in during the winter as I can. I believe it helps."

It sure helped us last year. He hit .280 with nine home runs after he came up on June 15. He even found himself in center field one day—a day when we put together one of the slowest outfields in baseball history.

I was in left. I can run. I'm no Lou Brock, but I did do 11.2 during the Superstars competition in the 100 and that isn't all bad.

But Kosco, a big, powerful guy, was in center, and our right-fielder was Johnny Bench.

That was against Pittsburgh and Bob Prince was announcing the game on the radio. Prince is a classic.

They say he actually dove out of the third-floor window into the swimming pool at the Chase Park Plaza Hotel in St. Louis. I've looked out from there and I can't believe it.

Anyway, about all Prince could think of to say about our outfield that day was, "Rose is the greyhound of that outfield."

March 29
Tampa

Opening day is a week away and I can't wait.

"Who's pitching for Atlanta opening day?" I say to Sparky as we stand by the batting cage.

"I guess Carl Morton," the Gray Fox answers.

"Ooooh. That means another fast start on a batting title. That's 3-for-4 at least."

Only Sparky could have pulled it off. It was the kind of thing that's made him famous. Do the impossible. Go against the book. Win.

I can remember one night in particular in 1972, a year when we were to win the pennant.

We were in Philadelphia, losing 2-0, when Tony Perez hit a one-out, run-scoring triple. That made it 2-1, not exactly caught up yet.

What did Sparky do? He ran Ted Uhlaender for Perez—took one of our biggest bats out of the lineup in an effort to tie the game, even though the Phils had three more trips to the plate.

Well, Uhlaender wound up dying at third, but we tied the game in the ninth and won it in the tenth. We won it when Uhlaender, hitting where Perez should have been hitting, got a single. It was one of eighteen hits he was to get all year.

Well, Sparky was at it again today. In the bottom of the ninth inning, we were trailing St. Louis, 3-1, with the bases loaded, one out, and pitcher Pedro Borbon due to hit.

Sparky had all the pinch hitters he could ever expect to have. What he didn't have was any pitchers left. He even called the minor league camp, but everyone was gone there.

Borbon had to hit and the Cardinals walked him. In

32

came a run. We scored another to tie the game and then we won it in the tenth on singles by me and Morgan and Bench's sacrifice fly.

Borbon's drawing a bases-loaded walk is nothing when you consider the character. This right-handed relief pitcher from the Dominican Republic is one of the biggest characters in baseball.

Remember the picture of him during the fight in the playoffs, ripping and biting Cleon Jones' hat to shreds?

Get this. Borbon swears his grandfather in the Dominican Republic is 136 years old. "He is the oldest man in the Dominican," he says in his halting English. "His name is Bernardo. He lives on the same street I do and he is blind and walks with a cane, but he gets around. Bernardo is the father of my mother. My father's father, he live only until he was 118. And his brother, he die at 102."

Borbon may exaggerate just a bit. Last year he told us his grandfather was 128. But who's counting?

There are pitchers in baseball who baby their arms, treat them like they were some delicate instrument. Not Borbon. The man has got the most amazing arm in baseball, and that includes Mike Marshall.

Borbon has had only one sore arm in his life and that, believe it or not, was his left arm, not his right.

"I was messing around in the outfield, throwing left-handed, and I hurt it," he once told me.

The only time Larry Starr, our trainer, sees Borbon is when he comes in to borrow a pair of scissors. He also happens to be a barber and cuts a lot of the guys' hair. Not mine. Mine looks bad enough as it is.

Borbon likes to use his arm to show off. In 1969 he stood at home plate in Boston's Fenway Park and threw a baseball on a fly to the center-field wall, more than 400 feet away.

Then, in 1972, he decided he could hit the ceiling in the

Astrodome and stood at second base trying to get one up there. He almost made it, too, until pitching coach Larry Shepard nearly had a heart attack and made him stop.

Borbon, they tell me, had this trick he'd perform when he was in the American Association. He would bet anyone that he could kneel in deepest center field, his feet against the wall, and throw the ball on a fly to second base.

"He had takers everywhere," pitcher Dick Baney told me. "And he won the bet every time."

They just don't make them like that any more, I guess.

April 1
Tampa

Tony Perez sat with his leg in the whirlpool, recovering from a pulled calf muscle. He hadn't played in five days and didn't figure to until opening day, now just four days off.

I looked in on him. As usual, he was all smiles and getting ready to put the needle in me. But I beat him to it.

"How can anyone who runs as slow as you pull a muscle?" I asked, sticking my head in the door of the training room.

His answer was in Spanish and it would be crude to translate it into English here.

April 2
Tampa

This is it. The final day of spring training. One more game and then it's on the big bird home. I can't wait.

I'd love to get a couple of hits today. It is kind of embarrassing to be the National League's batting champion and Most Valuable Player and not to be hitting your weight in spring training. And I only weigh 200 pounds.

Not that I'm worried. I was talking to Morgan about that today. He hasn't been hitting either and asked me about it.

"When we leave here and go back to Riverfront to open the season it will be the difference between night and day," I told him. "I know I'll hit once it starts for real. I don't see the ball real good down here and we've been facing more pitchers that I've never faced before than at any time I can remember. You know how that bothers me."

I really want to get off to a good start this year, maybe more than in any other season. Part of it has to do with the incident at the playoffs. Part, too, has to do with being MVP.

I don't know why, but everything I get has to be surrounded with controversy. When someone else wins the MVP award, everyone is happy. When I win it, they say Willie Stargell should have gotten it.

There are other reasons why I want to get going into the season, not just the personal reasons. I really believe this is our year. Losing the playoffs helped us grow up and that's just about all the Cincinnati Reds needed.

April 3
Tampa

Baseball isn't always a happy game. There are sad moments and I spent some time today thinking about that.

We open the season tomorrow and we're doing it without Dick Baney, Larry Stahl, Hal King, Joe Hague, and Gary Nolan.

Nolan's trying to make it back from that shoulder trouble with Indianapolis, but it isn't going to be long before

35

he requires surgery. Hague and Stahl, two veterans who knew their jobs and did them well, were released. It's awfully tough to catch on at this time of year, especially when you're a fringe player.

Hague wants to keep playing and has been talking to people in Mexico about playing in the Mexican League. Stahl probably will have to go back to the farm, although I understand the Giants are interested in him.

He took it pretty hard. Called me right after they told him they were going to turn him loose. "Why? Why?" he kept asking me. "Last year I did a good job for them. I can still hit and I can play the outfield and first base. Why? A year ago they wanted me badly. Now, nothing."

What can you say to a guy like that, a good guy who reaches the end of the line?

King and Baney, two guys who came up from Indianapolis in 1973 and helped us to the Western Division championship, went to Indy. I couldn't quite understand it with King.

Morgan was really disappointed about King's going down. "He was only the guy who won the pennant for us," Joe said. "A good guy, quiet, never did anything to hurt anyone. Just did his job, hit his home runs, and shut up. It's rotten."

Baney was another story. He had just gone through a terrible spring, and when Sparky called him in, he admitted it and made an unbelievably good impression on the manager.

"That," said Sparky after he cut Baney, "is the all-time man. I've met men before, but in 27 years in baseball, never anyone like him. He sat there, looked me right in the eye and said, 'I'm just happy to be in baseball. You're right sending me out. I was outpitched this spring. But I'm going down there and do the best I can.'

"Now that's a man. You run into 900 stories on why a

guy didn't pitch well. But not Baney. He really was something."

As I said, Sparky was impressed. I think Dick Baney will make it back with us.

April 4
Cincinnati

Opening day, 1974. The 99th opening day ever for the Cincinnati Reds. For Pete Rose, his twelfth. This is more than just a baseball game in Cincinnati. It's a holiday. The school kids get off. The bands come out. Parades. The whole works.

I still get a thrill out of opening day. Always will, I guess. This opener, though, is something else. For a change, it isn't the Reds who are in the spotlight. Instead it is the guy who wears No. 44 for the Atlanta Braves, the old guy in left field: Hank Aaron.

It seems kind of strange, playing a baseball game at all today. Just a day ago the Cincinnati area was overrun with tornadoes. The town of Xenia, Ohio, which is right outside Dayton, was half destroyed. People were killed; property damage was in the millions.

I saw the damn thing. It buzzed by my house not a block away, and let me tell you, I was scared. They tell me that Aaron saw it, too. He was out at the airport, to pick up his wife Billye, and the tornado was visible in the distance. It's a spooky feeling. But the game goes on and we played today.

Aaron, of course, came into the game with 713 home runs. Seems like every one of them was hit against the Reds. Actually, he had only 95 against the Reds, but that's more than he's hit against any other team.

A couple of days ago, seeing all the money being flashed around for home run balls numbers 714 and 715, I got to

37

thinking. It sure would be nice if Aaron's homer didn't carry into the stands, but just hit off the concrete wall and bounced back into play.

It would be one ball I wouldn't throw back into the stands. If some banker is going to give $10,000 to a kid in the stands, why not give it to me? And if he won't give it to me, I'll give the ball to my son and let him collect. After all, Magnavox has more money than Pete Rose.

I told that to a reporter; he wrote it and a guy named Julio Gonzalez, a businessman in Baltimore who has offered $15,000 for the ball, didn't like it.

"I think Pete Rose is making enough money," he said. "I don't think it would be very sporting of Pete to claim the money just by walking over and picking up the ball. After all, he is known as 'Charlie Hustle.' Now, if he'd grab the ball while falling over the fence, that would be something different."

We even have a guy like that in Cincinnati. His name is Charlie Jurgens. He's offering $12,000 for number 715 and he's running around the left-field stands with his son, 25 helpers, and two uniformed policemen. He needs the protection. He's carrying 120 crisp new $100 bills on him.

It is, of course, recorded history now that Henry Aaron hit his 714th home run against the Reds today. He did it against Jack Billingham, tying Babe Ruth's career record.

I couldn't quite believe it. He did it with the first swing of his bat, jumping on a 3-1 fast ball and sailing it over my head. I can still see that ball going up, up, and then out.

It hit the concrete wall, too, but bounced down behind the fence. They went wild and I stood there, frozen. Sure it was history, but it also was a three-run homer and we trailed, 3-0. That I didn't like.

And I didn't like, too, that it had to happen to Jack Billingham. Billingham is a tall, lazy-looking right-hander. But he can pitch. Last year he won nineteen games and he certainly doesn't deserve to be remembered for serving up number 714 to Hank Aaron.

Just to make matters worse, they stopped the game for a ceremony. Billingham, losing 3-0, and having given up THE home run, is standing out on the mound warming up.

Bowie Kuhn was there and so was Jerry Ford, then Vice-President of the United States.

I had met Ford before the game and he seemed like a helluva nice guy. "Maybe if I'd gone on and played for the Detroit Lions I would have made a name for myself," he laughed. He had been a center at the University of Michigan and could have played pro football.

He took a baseball signed by Johnny Bench and me and one of Bench's catcher's gloves signed by the team.

Later, they say, Ford, who played third base on the House of Representatives team, told people that "as an old, has-been athlete, I thoroughly enjoyed going into the locker room. I was impressed with the friendliness of the players. I was really struck with the friendliness of Pete Rose and Johnny Bench."

Ford congratulated Aaron on the home run, calling it "a great day for baseball."

Maybe so, but forces were working to make it seem something less. It all started a short time before the game. Aaron had spoken by telephone to the Reverend Jesse Jackson, who was in Memphis to eulogize the late Dr. Martin Luther King. Aaron figured it would be fitting, on the sixth anniversary of the assassination of Dr. King, to have a moment of silence before the game.

His request came too late, though, and the Reds had to turn it down. They probably would have anyway, according to the statement Dick Wagner, the Cincinnati vice-president, released.

"As a policy, our club has never gotten into religious things. We don't get into politics. We believe our fans come

39

to the ball park to be entertained. We don't do it for Kennedy, for Lincoln, or for anyone else. And it's not because of the men or what they stand for. We just don't think our fans want that at the ball park."

Aaron didn't like that a whole lot and neither did his wife Billye, who said, "It should not have been necessary to request a moment of silence. The stature of the man demanded it."

It was too bad that had to come up and ruin Aaron's moment. I had ruined it enough. We fought back from being down 6-2 to tie the game, 6-6, in the ninth inning. I drove in the tying run in the ninth inning. In the eleventh, I scored from second base on a wild pitch, making us 1-0 for the season. It was a great way to start a new season.

April 7
San Francisco

Jack Billingham got off the hook tonight. Henry Aaron got number 715. He did it the only way Aaron could do it, on the first swing of his bat in his home park in 1974. Al Downing was the victim.

I wish I could have been there to see it, but I did the next best thing. I watched it on television. I know Billingham was watching, too. He gave up 714 and he had to pitch again against Atlanta this week. He didn't want to be the man to give up both. He doesn't have to worry now.

I really don't believe people yet understand how great this record is that Aaron has set. It's a record that will never be broken. And Henry isn't through. He will probably finish with 740 homers or so for his career, and that's if he sticks to it and quits at the end of the season.

Figure it out. If a guy comes into the league and plays twenty years, he has to average 35 homers a year to reach 700. And that still leaves him a year and a half short of

40

breaking the mark. Who, though, is going to play twenty years? I may be the last guy in baseball ever to reach that, if I hold out like I think I will. With all the money guys are making now, they don't have to play twenty years. The young, modern players just aren't doing it.

No, Aaron's record is safe. It takes nothing away from Ruth's mark. Ruth's record still is fantastic. So is Henry's.

April 9
San Francisco

We're playing the Giants today and they have Gary Matthews in left field, the National League's Rookie of the Year. He brings back memories. Ten years earlier, a brash, cocky, crew-cut kid was named Rookie of the Year. Me.

I had what you'd call a helluva rookie season. Scored 101 runs. Hit .273. Got 170 hits and that's a lot for a rookie. Matthews, for example, had 162 hits and he batted .300.

But my rookie season in the big leagues, 1963, was anything but a fun year. Oh, sure, I was up in the clouds. It took me a couple of years to come down. In fact, I was so high I hardly realized what was going on. The guys on my team—the white guys—didn't like me.

It had all started in an exhibition game during spring training. I was a second baseman and stood about as much chance of making the team as a rookie left-fielder would have of beating me out today. Don Blasingame was the second baseman and he had just completed the best season of his life. He hit .281 and seemed set to go.

So one day we're playing an exhibition game and Fred Hutchinson tells us we can take off. I'm about ready to leave when Mike Ryba, a coach who died a couple of years ago—he fell out of a tree during the winter—turns to me. "Why don't you stick around, kid," he says. "You might get to play."

41

So I stick around and the first thing you know it's the eleventh inning and I get to pinch-run. Sure enough, someone drives me in and the game is tied again. I have a chance to hit and I get a double. Still tied. So I hit again and double again. This time someone gets a hit, I score and we win.

Now Hutch likes the fact that I stayed around and likes what I did, and he starts playing me. I'm loving it, but the guys on the team aren't. This was a team of cliques, and guys like Gene Freese, Eddie Kasko, and Bob Purkey don't like it. They won the pennant in 1961 with Blasingame at second and they feel they can win it again, but with him, not me, there.

Besides, I didn't fit in. I was one of those kids who didn't have a coat or tie. All I wore was alpaca sweaters. If Sparky had been managing, I couldn't have made the team. He has a rule that you have to wear a coat and tie on the airplane. Anyway, it becomes obvious that I'm going to play second base for the Cincinnati Reds. We go to Mexico City and I go 2-for-25. Now we return to Vero Beach to play the Dodgers and I'm still in the lineup. That's when it got through these guys' heads that Hutch liked me and was going to keep me in the lineup.

So now they start avoiding me. I have no one to run with except for Frank Robinson and Vada Pinson. That's why I have so much respect for those guys today. They treated me like a human being.

We go into the season and I'm a lost soul. I remember one night we were in Chicago. It was about five after twelve when I got in and I went to my room. The door was locked. My roommate, Jim Coates, had the door locked and he wouldn't open it. So I went upstairs and slept with Vada. He roomed with Frank then, but Robinson was in Cincinnati having his arm worked on.

The next morning Vada bought me room service. First

time I ever had room service. It was about $12 for breakfast and he picked up the check. I'll always remember that.

The next day I saw Coates, but I didn't say anything to him, other than how come you had the chain on. I didn't want to bother him. I was just a kid and he had his own problems.

Well, this goes on all year. Finally Bill DeWitt, who owned the Reds, calls me into his office. He wants to talk to me about hanging around with Vada and Frank. I guess Hutch told him I was hanging around with the black players too much and he didn't want me getting a reputation.

"They're the only ones who treat me like a human being," I tell DeWitt. "Besides, I don't look at them as black or white. They're just teammates and friends. Hell, you don't look at a man's skin color. He's a person."

Actually, DeWitt's talk couldn't have accomplished anything. It wasn't me who was avoiding the white players. They didn't want to hang around with me. It stuck like that all year, too. The next season Hutch came down with cancer and things changed a little, and the following year we started getting new players, the guys I knew like Tommy Helms and Tony Perez and Chico Ruiz, and Dave Bristol came up to coach. That's when things started getting better.

Anyway, those are the things I remember as I stand here in Candlestick Park and watch Gary Matthews take batting practice. I know it had to be easier on him.

Today the Giants were on the spot. We beat them, 6-3, to end a two-game losing streak, and I had three hits.

April 10
San Francisco

Somewhere along the way, I've heard this charming city by the bay described as "The Paris of the West."

43

Sophisticated? Lovely? Filled with charm and excitement?

Bull.

Candlestick Park is a sad excuse for a ball park. It might just be the coldest spot on earth. And certainly it's the windiest. Who can forget Stu Miller being blown off the pitcher's mound during the 1961 All-Star game?

At one time it was almost impossible to play here. The wind blew so hard that you had to hit a screamer to left field to get it out while a routine pop would go out over the right-field wall.

And try this sometime. It's 50 degrees and the wind is blowing right in your face. You're at the plate, waiting to hit and Juan Marichal is pitching for the Giants. Marichal stands there and stands there and stands there until your eyes start to water. That's when he goes into his motion and pitches.

At first they had grass here, the most beautiful grass in the league. Trouble was the San Francisco Forty-Niners moved over here to play so they installed AstroTurf. One good feature in the whole damn park and they change it.

The wind would whip endlessly, blowing dirt and hot dog wrappers, and the fans, what few of them there were, would be bundled in blankets and warm jackets. The players would be huddled together, trying to keep warm.

Unbelievable. Down the coast twenty miles the temperature might be 86 degrees and at Candlestick, 50.

The park is uncomfortable. If you have the best seat in the house, front row, you have to walk up 2,000 stairs to get to a rest room or a concession stand.

Is it any wonder, then, that the fans stay away? And is it any wonder that the ones who come act miserably?

I don't know what I'd do if I were sitting in the stands with my wife and kids and my mother and someone were yelling some of the things they yelled at me during this three-game series.

Sports are funny. People think that when they pay their money to get in, they can do anything they want. There's not a whole lot that can be done about it, either. The cops aren't making much money and they aren't armed. Certainly the usherettes can't handle a 250-pound goon who's shouting and throwing things.

I just don't understand it. Why me? The fight with Harrelson last year? What the hell does that have to do with the people here? My beating out Bobby Bonds last year for Most Valuable Player? I didn't vote.

Yet they boo me and throw things at me in San Francisco. A couple of days ago, they were cheering for Cesar Cedeno, the Houston outfielder, and he was involved in a lot messier thing than I was—a shooting during the winter.

To be honest, I don't mind the boos. I kind of like them. I know I'd rather be here playing ball than be home listening to the game on the radio. And when I'm booed, I normally react.

I know Sparky Anderson just told a reporter that "I hope they keep booing him all year."

From the looks of it, they will. Meanwhile, I'll just have to keep right on going my way and doing my thing. My thing was five hits in thirteen tries during this series and that isn't all bad. No wonder Sparky wants them to keep booing me.

Maybe they ought to boo all the Reds. We lost, 4-3.

April 12
Atlanta

Today I got word that the World Baseball League, something that so far is nothing but a fantasy, wants to give me $100,000 in cash and $200,000 a year for five years to jump to its team in Columbus.

45

We checked on it and we can't even find a team in Columbus or a World Baseball League, even though they have gotten some ink in the newspapers.

To tempt me to sign something like that would take a whole lot more than they offered. Hell, it would take damn near that much to get me to approve a trade. As a ten-year man, all that time with the Reds, they must ask my approval before they trade me.

Believe me, I'd have to contact the people I'm being traded to before I'd okay the deal. That happened this winter with Ron Santo. The Cubs traded him to California and he said, "No thanks." He demanded they send him to the White Sox and that's what they wound up doing.

I have to have some security, too. I wouldn't sign with any other team unless I got a three-year contract. At this stage in my career, I'm looking for security.

For another league to have any chance of working, they would have to do away with baseball's reserve clause so that a player could play out his option and become a free agent. That would be horrible. Even though it's been challenged over and over, Curt Flood being the last to do so, it hasn't been done away with and that's good. Baseball needs some form of control like that.

Otherwise, some millionaire will buy up all the good players and win everything. That can't be.

Besides, who wants to leave Cincinnati when you win easy games like today's 14-2 laugher over the Braves. I got three hits and now have two or more hits in five of our first seven games.

April 14
Atlanta

Tony Perez hit a home run today. It didn't count. We got rained out.

Damn rain. You come to Atlanta and you can count on it, just like you can count on seeing some beautiful women on Peachtree Street.

We're sitting around the clubhouse during the delay and Andy Kosco, who has been around so much he has stories about everyone, is telling his favorite rainy day story.

"I'm with Milwaukee," begins Kosco, who also has been with Detroit, Minnesota, California, the Dodgers, and the Yankees. "Jim Lonborg is pitching against the Tigers and it's raining like hell. He's got the lead and is in the fifth inning. Needs three outs to make it an official game.

"He goes out to the mound and is rushing. Del Crandall, the manager, decides he'd better go out and tell him to slow down and get the side out. No sooner does he get back to the dugout than it really rains.

"The game's stopped. The delay is about an hour and a half. Now they start play again and Lonborg goes to the mound. The first guy singles. The second guy walks. The third guy singles.

"Crandall figures he'd better steady the big guy down and goes out for a talk. All of a sudden Billy Martin is shouting from the Tiger dugout. 'That's his second trip to the mound this inning. He's gotta take the pitcher out.'

"Sure enough, Crandall had forgotten that first trip before the rain. Lonborg's got to go and Milwaukee has no one warming up. They bring a guy in totally cold, he gets belted and Lonborg is stuck with a loss. I mean he's mad.

"Next day, a pitcher gets in trouble. Crandall decides he'd better go out and talk to him. He bounces to his feet and falls flat on his face.

" 'You ain't going nowhere,' laughs Lonborg, who somehow slipped down behind Crandall and tied his feet together."

The Houston Astros are in town for the first time this year and that's cause for celebration. Now in my mind and most of our minds, the Astros are the team we have to fear most. But somehow it's a friendly kind of rivalry. How could it be any different with Tommy Helms and Lee May on the other side?

Tommy Helms and I grew up together. I just about lived with him from the time I was 17 until the winter of 1971. That's when Bob Howsam stunned me and the rest of the baseball world by engineering that eight-player trade with Houston.

We got Joe Morgan, Jack Billingham, Denis Menke, Cesar Geronimo and Ed Armbrister. But we gave up Helms and May and Jimmy Stewart.

I couldn't believe it when that trade was announced. I guess I was thinking like everybody else. I know nobody in Cincinnati liked the deal when it was made. I knew Morgan was a good player and Menke was a good player and Billingham could pitch and Geronimo had potential. But May and Helms?

What I didn't realize, and I hadn't played on AstroTurf enough to realize, was that Howsam was going for speed and defense. Now I can understand that catching the ball and throwing the ball and stealing a base are more helpful to a team than home runs . . . at least on the turf.

Baseball can be a sad time, though, especially when your friends are traded. Hell, the saddest time is in spring training when you see a guy with kids get released. That really hurts.

After all, I lived with Helms from the time I got out of high school. I loved him. And I was with Lee May a long time. Then the first thing I know, they're both gone.

People don't realize it, but there are a lot of inner feelings in a game, far beyond the 0-for-4's and the 3-for-4's. There's a lot of sentiment and friendship. You become one family and then boom, it's broken up.

You have to adjust, become a bit cold. You can't worry about it, because it happens every year. You just have to realize that the money is just as green in California and Texas as it is in Cincinnati. You have to realize this is nothing but a job.

Somehow, though, that's hard to do.

I think back to that trade and how it made the Reds. It brought us Morgan, who has been virtually the most valuable player in the league in 1972 and 1973, even though he hasn't won the award. Billingham has been our top pitcher. And Geronimo is blossoming.

But all of a sudden, May and Helms were gone. Tommy Helms, gone.

What times we had together. I remember one night we're in Houston and this girl has this big birthday party for him. She was one of those society chicks. Her sister was in the Miss Texas contest. In fact, her sister wound up marrying Larry Dierker of the Astros, although they're now divorced.

Anyway she's having this big, formal party. What does Tommy do? He goes out with Jim Owens, who was then pitching coach for the Astros. He doesn't even show up for his own birthday party.

Worse yet, for some reason, he's mad at her.

I'm just sitting in my room when she comes over and she's got this big birthday cake.

"Can I leave it for Tommy?" she asks.

"Sure, thanks," I say. "Set it down."

She leaves. A little later, Tommy walks in. He takes the damn cake and throws it up against the wall in the room, right over my bed, and it looks like it's going to drop, but it

49

doesn't. It just sticks there against the wall. So we have to get chairs up on the bed and scrape the damn cake off the wall so it doesn't fall on me when I'm sleeping.

That's how it was with Tommy, but Howsam traded him and Lee May and I'm wondering why. I didn't realize what the hell was going on.

May had just come off a 39-homer season. But that's how Howsam operates. He probably could have traded Tony Perez instead of May, but he might not have gotten Armbrister. Tony had gone through a year that was not his best. So Howsam got an extra player for Lee May.

He trades good personnel and gets away with it. Look at the list of guys he's traded: Hal McRae, Ross Grimsley, Ed Sprague, Alex Johnson, George Culver, Tommy Helms, Lee May, Vada Pinson, Johnny Edwards. That's why everyone says he's a good trader. He has good personnel to trade and he's not afraid to do it. He gets what he wants because he doesn't cheat people.

So now, for the third straight year, Tommy Helms and I are on different sides of the fence. I hope he comes in second.

He came in first today. The Astros whipped us, 5-3. For the first time this year we're under .500 at 4-5. No one's worried.

April 17
Cincinnati

As I said, Tommy Helms wasn't the only guy I hated to see leave us back in 1971 when Howsam engineered the deal that got us Morgan. Lee May was leaving and he's one of those once-in-a-lifetime ballplayers.

Nothing bothers him. He's happy-go-lucky, dedicated, quiet, and a winner.

There is, in fact, only one strange thing about Lee May. He wears a toupee. Before he had it, as his hair was slipping further and further back you could see he had one of those heads that came to a point. I mean it was really bad. One night he was sliding into second base, trying to break up a double play. The shortstop made the throw, and as he followed through, he hit May right on top of that pointed head. Perez couldn't wait for him to get back to the dugout.

"Hey, Mo," said Tony, using May's nickname. "It's a wonder that guy didn't cut his hand off on that head of yours."

May has always been super-conscious of his hair. One Friday when he was with the Reds, he got his hair cut and, to be honest, the guy butchered it. It was bad and Lee knew it.

For three days, he refused to take his hat off. He waited until the anthem was played before he'd go to his position. When he batted, he wore his hat under his helmet so he didn't have to take his helmet off to put on his hat. He is the only guy I remember in a Cincinnati uniform to do that. We have a rule against it, but Sparky waived it; otherwise Lee might not have played.

Then there was the night we were playing against the Giants and Lee came racing home from second base. There was a big collision at the plate and May was safe. Trouble was, he didn't get up. Just lay there in the dirt. Everyone figured he was hurt and ran to home plate.

"I'm all right. I'm all right," he said. "I'm just feeling to make sure my rug is on."

Lee May was proud of one thing other than his store-bought hair. "Nobody can get me loaded," he'd pronounce; then he would drink anyone under the table who tried.

He can't make that boast any more. I got him drunk at a party of mine. "See that guy over there," I said to the

51

bartender, pointing to May. "He says no one can get him loaded. Every time he asks for a drink, you triple up on the scotch and hold the water."

He did, and Lee kept right on drinking. The hours passed and he finally left. He jumped in the car, started to drive off, and wound up on the curb. "Well, Pete did it," he said to his wife Teri. "You drive home from here."

Old Mo is quite a guy. And I figure I might as well talk about him today. It beats talking about the game. Houston beat us, 14-1, our third loss in a row. You can bet May is out celebrating tonight.

April 20
Cincinnati

I must admit, I have had worse days than this. To begin with, we beat the San Diego Padres for the second day in a row. The score was 11-0 and Don Gullett pitched the shutout.

The day was more than that. I contributed my first four-hit day of the season. My batting average stands at .407 and I'm as mystified about it as anyone.

I'm not supposed to hit in April. I've had only two good Aprils in my life. I don't like the cold weather and I'm seeing a lot of pitchers for the first time.

Believe me, I'm not complaining. I'd like nothing better than to win a fourth batting title, although that is not a goal of mine. I have to start thinking about it, though. A start like this can knock you right off your feet.

When you swing the bat like I am, all kinds of heavy thoughts go through your mind. Like can you hit .400?

I have the answer to that. No one will ever hit .400 again. Believe me when I say that. Consider me. I'm a pretty good hitter. But I also play every day. I'm a lead-off batter. I go to bat five times a game. Over a season I'll have about 650

52

at-bats. To hit .400 with that many at-bats I would need 260 hits. That would be a record. No one has ever gotten that many and I have no thoughts that I will.

Night ball and the travel work against a .400 hitter, too. No matter what anyone tells you, it's harder to see the ball at night than during the day. And the travel is ridiculous. There must be a better way of scheduling than the one they have now.

Later this year, in August, we have an interesting little trip. We play on a Wednesday night in Cincinnati, then fly after the game to San Francisco. We'll get to Frisco at about 1:30 A.M. coast time, which is 4:30 A.M. body time. That night we play in San Francisco. The next night we play there again. That is Friday, and after the game we fly to San Diego.

Very nice, a Saturday off. Seems they have a football game in the stadium Saturday night so we can't play. They make up for it, though, with a Sunday doubleheader. After that, it's off to Los Angeles, by bus. In L.A. we play three games, the first one starting on Monday at 5:15 P.M., for national television. Wonderful. Hitting at 5:15 P.M., with the shadows that are being cast, is like trying to swat flies with a string of spaghetti.

Following Wednesday night's game, we have a day off. That should be very relaxing. At noon we climb on board a commercial 747 and fly to New York, arriving at 8:00 P.M. New York time. By now, though, our bodies are accustomed to coast time and we have to readjust.

We start off with a night game at Shea Stadium, then follow it with two day games. And people expect us to hit .400. Ha!

"Hitting is the hardest individual thing there is in sports," Ted Williams said, and he was the last .400 hitter.

I believe him, I believe him. But, right now, let me enjoy my .407 average. I know it won't last.

This morning we flew from Cincinnati. Just another flight in the life of a baseball player, who seems to be forever going to or coming from some airport. Flying becomes second nature for most of us, until something happens. And I've had my share of close calls.

We were flying out of Milwaukee one time when we looked out the window and the damn engine was on fire. They had to shut it down and make an emergency landing. Scared? Everyone was.

And then there was the time we were in Houston and blowing down the runway about to take off. We had just about passed the point of no return when all of a sudden the brakes went on and we raced like hell to get off the runway. We made it just before another plane made a landing on the same runway.

I remember that one because they made us go back to the gate. The air conditioner wasn't working and we sat there for 45 minutes, drowning in our own sweat.

About the worst flight I ever had was one leaving spring training to go to New Orleans. It was one giant thunderstorm all the way, the plane behaving like a knuckle ball. About eight of us, including me, got sick and were tossing our cookies everywhere.

I don't worry much on an airplane, except when we have to circle New York, Chicago, or L.A. I know what kind of traffic there is there and I'd just as soon never fly into those places.

I get a little edgy, too, flying out of the airports in those cities. There are a lot of kooky people in those towns and a lot of crazy things happen around the airports.

It's amazing that no pro team has ever gone down in a

plane crash. When you think of all the teams flying and how many miles they all put in, you have to wonder.

Some guys, of course, never get over being scared on an airplane. About the worst I ever saw was Wayne Simpson, the pitcher who won thirteen of his first fourteen decisions for us in 1970. He'd sit there and just squeeze away on those seats from the time we took off until we landed. And usually he needed a few good belts of scotch to make the flight even more comfortable.

Hal King is another of those guys who hates to go up in the air. He would spend most of his time up in the cockpit of the charter with the pilot. "I just want to make sure they don't do nothing wrong," he reasoned.

"Can you fly?" I asked him.

"Hell no," he answered.

"Then how will you know if anything's wrong?" I asked.

"I won't," he said. "But they don't know that."

Whenever we hit an air pocket, I'd run after King. "We're going down. We're going down," I'd yell, and he'd really get scared. "We're going down and I have a .300 lifetime average to take with me. Do you?"

We once had a rebellion on an airplane. It was 1971 and we were going from Miami to Venezuela to play some exhibition games with the Pittsburgh Pirates. To begin with, we had to check out of our hotel rooms at 1:00 P.M., but the flight wasn't scheduled until 8:00. That left a lot of drinking time for the boys and they took advantage of it.

When we got to the airport, we found out there was a delay. More drinking time. By the time we were ready to leave, about midnight, there were some players who could have flown to Venezuela without a plane. As we were boarding, Ted Uhlaender, who flies his own plane, overheard the pilot talking to the steward in Spanish.

Uhlaender spoke Spanish and what he heard was that

55

the plane was overloaded, but that they were going to try to make it anyway. That was all he had to hear.

"I ain't going," he said, as he led a procession of ballplayers off the plane. Bench got off and so did Carroll and Simpson, among others. It finally took Sparky to order them back on before we flew to Venezuela.

Today's flight offered no problems, though. There were the usual card games—Sparky and Joe Nuxhall in the front playing hearts against Morgan and Larry Shepard. Sparky and Nux are just overmatched.

The ballgame didn't offer any problems, either. We won, 4-3.

April 27
St. Louis

Hal McCoy is a writer for the Dayton *Daily News* who travels with us. On the road, every day, he puts on his tennis outfit, grabs a racquet and heads for the court.

He has absolutely fallen in love with the game. They tell me he's become a pretty good player, too. Today one of the other writers approached me with the idea of playing tennis with McCoy. Some of the guys are ready to put up a few bucks.

"I have the feeling I'm getting hustled," I say. I should know. I've played against the greatest hustler of them all. It was Charlie Hustle versus The Happy Hustler: Pete Rose versus Bobby Riggs.

I'd been playing tennis for only a couple of months, getting ready for the Superstars' competition. I had become decent at the game and the match was for charity.

Bobby Riggs knows what it's all about. He figures he made a million and a half from his match with Billie Jean King.

This is show business and Riggs is playing his role: a 55-year-old man who has the teenage girls giggling and coming up for a kiss. Put a microphone in front of him and he goes right to it.

"Really, I like women. I like them so much I think every man should own two. They love to kiss me and run their fingers through my hair. That's why I grow my hair long like Pete Rose. I'd like to play Billie Jean again. Ali reversed the decision on Frazier in a second fight, and that's what would happen if I played Billie Jean again.

"But the one I really want is Rosie Casals. She's the one who said I'm so old I can't see and can't hear. She's the one who said I'd think Billie Jean was an amateur after playing her."

On and on until it was time for tennis. Riggs served. He spun one that barely cleared the net then bounced crazily off to one side.

"Serve like a man," I shouted, knowing I'm in for some night. I made a good shot, over my head with my back to the net on one of his deep lobs. He returned and I had an easy drop shot. I blew it.

Into the air went my racquet. I knew I couldn't beat him, but I didn't want to embarrass myself. I just wanted to keep the ball in play so he could put on a show.

And that's just what he did. He played me wearing a dress, carrying a parasol, and with two chairs set up on his side of the court, yelling, "I just want Rose to see how I felt when I had to play a woman."

He added chairs, put on a raincoat, and carried a suitcase. He played in a heavy winter coat and with boots on and wearing full catcher's gear, mask and all.

"I once gave a banker in Texas 32 chairs and beat him for $10,000," Riggs said.

He beat me, too, although I did win a couple of games. When it was over, I had one thing left to do. There was a little crippled girl at courtside. Doctors said she had only a year to live. I went over, talked to her, signed an autograph. The night was worthwhile.

April 28
St. Louis

We're playing the Cardinals today and Bob Gibson is pitching. Now some pitchers are good and some are lucky. Gibson is good. At everything. But I'm reminded of Tim McCarver's line.

McCarver is back with the Cardinals now. Last year, though, when he was playing at Montreal, the conversation got around to lucky pitchers. "Gibson's the luckiest pitcher I've ever seen," Tim said.

"Oh, yeah. Why?" he was asked.

"Because he always picks the night to pitch when the other team doesn't score any runs."

Well, Gibby picked the right night to pitch this time. Clay Kirby started for us and just didn't have it. We got him a run in the first when I doubled, Morgan walked, and Danny Driessen doubled.

If you're going to beat Gibson, you have to get him early and it looked like we might do it. Another walk loaded the bases with two out, but Gibby worked free.

The Cards came back and got him four runs in the first, three in the second, and two in the third. After three innings, it was 9-1 and St. Louis had thirteen hits.

That was all they needed. And, dammit all, I was swinging the bat good. After my first-inning double, I hit two singles, then a line drive right back at Gibson into a double play. I hit that one hard enough to be my fourth hit.

So we were out of the game in the ninth when I came up and Gibson threw one that just nicked me. Now I was swinging so well I didn't want to go to first base and was almost arguing with the umpire that the ball didn't hit me.

But I had to go to first. I just wonder if Gibson felt I was showing him up. If so, I wonder if he'll remember it the next time we meet.

Oh, well, such is life.

April 30
Pittsburgh

No game today. Rain. That means time on your hands in the hotel and that isn't all bad. It gives you a chance to think, and being in Pittsburgh, I do a lot of thinking.

Tonight, I'm thinking about Fred Hutchinson and Irma the Body. Maybe you heard of Irma. She was a famous stripper. I think her real name was Elizabeth Goodneighbor.

Anyway it's my rookie year and I'm over at Frankie Gustine's restaurant having a bite to eat. I'm a rookie, not wearing a coat, just an alpaca sweater. I'm sitting there and Irma's at the next table, dressed all sexy and everything like those strippers do.

We get to talking. She asks me do I want to come see her show. Now I've never seen a strip show before, so I say sure. And she says we can work out a deal.

"You get me tickets for the baseball game and I'll leave you tickets for the strip show."

Okay, I say, and the next afternoon—it's a Saturday—I leave her tickets. I remember we're taking batting practice before the game. I'm out in center field and I see her walk up to the dugout.

She's got on the sexiest damn outfit that I've ever seen. And she's got the biggest breasts in the world—48 or 50D.

59

Hutch is standing in the dugout and she looks at him and says, "Hey, No. 1. No. 1."

He turns around and is stunned.

"Which one's Rose?" she asks, and his tongue almost drops out.

I mean she's about 40 years old, with these breasts, and I'm a rookie and he thinks I'm playing around with her.

"Rose, get in here," he shouts and I come in in a hurry.

"What the hell's going on?" he asks.

I explain the deal I made for the tickets and that I'd never seen a strip show and he's laughing his ass off.

A year later, Hutch is dying from cancer and it's one of the saddest sights you've ever seen. This was a man's man, and he expected everyone around him to be a man.

He'd fight anyone, come to the ball park with sunglasses on because his eye was black under it and he didn't want anyone to know. Just a helluva guy and he's dying from cancer right before our eyes and we can't take it.

It's 1964 and we want to win for him and almost do and then blow the damn thing the last day of the season.

Anyway, Hutch is sick and a year has gone by and we're at Forbes Field. I look up and here comes Irma the Body. Sexy as hell. She's got a poodle in one hand.

In the other is a balloon and all it says is, "We Love Hutch."

I'll never forget it. She must have read about his cancer in the paper and she went to the trouble to do that.

Those, I guess, are the kind of things you're supposed to think about when you're rained out in Pittsburgh.

May 1
Pittsburgh

Well, the rain let up enough to let us get a game in tonight, and that I like. Off-days are miserable, especially on the road.

No batting practice and I can't hit without batting practice.

I was a little worried going into this one. Just wondered about the reception I'd get from the Pittsburgh fans. Last November, you see, I was named the Most Valuable Player in the National League.

The man I edged out was Willie Stargell of the Pirates. A lot of people thought he deserved it. I didn't. I thought I deserved it.

Willie and I spoke about it this spring and there were no hard feelings as far as he was concerned. But how would the fans react in Pittsburgh?

The year Joe Torre was named the MVP, Stargell finished second and thought he should have won it. So did a lot of people.

But you've got to consider what the MVP award really is. It isn't an award for the best ballplayer. It's for "the most valuable player," and that can carry a lot of meaning. To me it is something other than just statistics or home runs. It's what you do off the field, too. They say I had more to do for the Reds last year off the field than I did on it. I hope they're right. I do know that all of a sudden people are looking at me as a leader, and I try to be one. I like to think I had something to do with the way the kids performed for us.

I know I went out of my way to help the youngsters— Dan Driessen, Ken Griffey, George Foster, Dick Baney. I try to make them feel like big leaguers. I think, too, that I had something to do with Joe Morgan's performance. He keeps saying I do. When he was at Houston he hit .260. Here he hits almost .300 and I like to think that I'm part of the reason.

I help him on the field because, hitting second, he has me at first base a lot. That means the first baseman is holding me on base and he has a bigger hole to shoot for on the right side. Off the field I think I've helped because I've let him know what it means to go 100 percent all the time. He always had a tendency, in a game where he was losing 10-0 or winning 10-0, not to concentrate. If he got two hits his first two times up, he wouldn't bear down the third. I think I inspired him to go all out all the way. I hope I had something to do with it. If only I could get through to every player as I have to Morgan, we'd have a much better team.

Leadership is important. I lead by doing. I think the guys are inspired when they see me take an extra base, smash into a catcher, dive in the outfield. My playing like that shows up guys who aren't hustling. And guys who aren't hustling don't like to be shown up. But I believe in only one way of playing the game. That is all the way. Nothing short will do.

In 1973, for example, we were going badly. We couldn't win for trying and the Dodgers kept pulling further and further away. I came down with a severe muscle pull in my leg. Sparky wanted to sit me down. He was afraid I might aggravate it and be out a couple of months. "Sparky, you can't sit me down," I said. "Morgan's already out with an injury. You know what other teams try to do to us. They try to keep me and Joe off base. If we're both in the dugout, there's no way we can get on." I played and we snapped out of it.

I like to think those kind of things are the reason I was named MVP, not just because I got 230 hits or led the league in hitting.

Anyway, the crowd in Pittsburgh didn't have much of a chance to boo me on this night. Dock Ellis saw to that.

I came up and he threw one at my head. He missed. So he threw another and this one hit me. Then he hit Morgan. Then he hit Driessen. A record. The first three batters in the game hit by the pitch.

Next was Perez. Dock threw at him and missed, finally walking him. Now Bench. He threw at him and missed. With the count 2-and-0, old Dock had himself a shower.

He had thrown twelve pitches. Not one of them was a strike. He hit three, walked one. We wound up winning 5-3, so it was a good night all the way around.

Today we got to hear all about Ray Shore's scouting report on the Chicago Cubs. Shore is our super scout, analyzing upcoming opponents for two very important reasons.

The first reason is to have information for the future. Come trade time, he is probably the most important man in the organization other than Bob Howsam, because he's seen the other players in the National and American Leagues. He has rated them all.

The second reason is to give us a report on the team we play next.

To be honest, I don't like the scouting reports. They are just like every meeting I've ever attended. Pitch this guy up and in, low and away. Hell, that's how you'd pitch Jesus Christ if He was hitting.

If I was running a meeting or turning in a scouting report, it would say things like never throw Bobby Bonds a fast ball and I don't give a damn what the situation is. I'd never throw Bobby Tolan a strike on the first pitch. He'll chase bad pitches.

I'd make my pitcher bear down and never walk Manny Sanguillen and the same goes for Tito Fuentes. Those guys should never walk.

There's another reason I don't like scouting reports. They really don't say anything to me. I would like it much better if they compared pitchers to other guys who I know. I don't want to know that Bill Bonham has a good change-up.

I want to know it's like Gary Nolan's change-up. I want to know this guy's fast ball is like Tom Griffin's. That would help.

I find I can depend on the word of other players much more than I can on the report. Even guys from the other teams will tell you what a rookie throws and who he's like.

Of course, that can backfire sometimes. I used to get Gordy Coleman in all kinds of trouble. I'm a switch-hitter and a guy never really looks like he's blowing it in there to me. I'd face a pitcher and Gordy would come to me and say, "What's he throw?"

"His fast ball is pretty straight and he isn't throwing much."

Sure enough, Gordy would walk up there and psst, psst, psst, the guy would blow Gordy away and he'd come back and say the pitcher's throwing the hell out of the ball.

It depends, too, on how you're swinging the bat. If you're swinging well and are quick, nothing looks tough to hit. That happened last night. Bench asked me what a guy was throwing and I told him his fast ball wasn't much and he was throwing a lot of hard sliders.

So Bench struck out on some change-up sliders and he came back and said, "Damn, you didn't tell me about that pitch." I guess I messed him up.

Scouting reports are helpful because they give you some up-to-date information about injuries, guys who can't throw, etc. They'll tell you, for example, that Jimmy Wynn can't throw. So now you have to try to hit the ball to him so you can have a chance to take an extra base. That will foul you up.

And guess what happens with nine out of ten players. They'll know his arm is hurting and hit a blooper to center, take the big turn, but not go to second. In the heat of the action, they'll forget the report.

The report wasn't much help to us today, although this was a game we should have won. We were losing, 4-2, going into the ninth inning, and I hit a three-run homer.

I was really high, flying around the bases, clapping my hands. This had to be a one-run win for us. You're not supposed to lose when Pete Rose hits three-run homers in the ninth.

But Don Gullett came out of the bullpen, walked Vic Harris, and let Rick Monday hit one into the left-center field bleachers. What a helpless feeling that is, watching the ball sail over your head and into the seats to end the game.

Gullett really took this loss hard, too. First time I've ever seen it get to him. He had to go out to dinner tonight with Fred Norman, who talked to him pretty good. Losers have to forget.

May 4
Chicago

It happened again. Hard as it is to believe, it happened again. This time it was Norman, who last night played big brother to Gullett. We were leading 2-0 in the ninth inning, one out, and a ground ball was hit to Darrel Chaney, our defensive replacement at third. That's a tough job, to go in cold and make all the plays.

This play Chaney didn't make. He threw the ball away and the Cubs scored twice in the ninth to tie it.

Norman came on to pitch and retired the first five men he faced. He threw one pitch to Billy Williams, a pitch Williams was looking for, and Billy hit it six miles over the center-field wall.

We lost, 3-2. When are we going to stop giving games away?

I felt sorry for Freddie Norman tonight. I also felt sorry for Satch Davidson, the third-base umpire.

Norman lost a game he never should have lost. Davidson got hit in the back with a full, unopened beer can.

Little Freddie, who is 5-foot-8—and all of it heart—wound up striking out thirteen Cardinals. He walked only one. He gave up only six hits. He lost, 1-0.

It was the ninth inning. Reggie Smith, who has been some kind of addition for the Cardinals, led off with a single. Then Freddie decided to get cute. He tried a pickoff, and before we knew it, Smith was at second on a wild throw.

"Hell," Freddie said later. "I can throw home and I can't throw to first."

A ground ball got Smith to third and Joe Torre brought him home. That was it as Lynn McGlothen, who came over from Boston as did Smith, pitched a four-hitter.

But, as has been happening so damn much this year, the fans stole the show from one of the better games of the season. First it was this joker running out on the field in the eighth inning.

He skips across the outfield like a 9-year-old kid heading for the candy store. He gets to the center-field wall and stands there, arms spread and head bowed, looking like some kind of Jesus freak.

The cops come and he tries to get away. No go. They cuff him. Still he isn't cooperating. He's battling all the way, refusing to walk. And all the while the fans are cheering him.

Big deal, this kid. The cops can't just bop him, even though he is resisting arrest. It takes them ten minutes to drag him from the field.

We're just about ready to start play again when, from deep in the blue seats, this beer can hits Davidson right in the small of the back. Ken Reitz, the Cardinal third baseman, immediately starts shouting at the people in the stands.

"You're sick," he says. "It's people like you who make things like this happen."

"What's wrong with that?" shouts back one big mouth. "He's only an umpire."

I couldn't believe it. Only an umpire. Aren't umpires human beings, too?

Ed Sudol, the crew chief, is in a fit of rage. "What the hell happens if that hits him in the temple?" he asks. "It's a damn tragedy, that's what. One more incident and I'm pulling the teams off the field."

There were no more incidents. In fact, the fans pointed out the coward who threw the beer. He was arrested and charged with assault.

I hope they throw the book at him. You've got to get tough with the clowns who are throwing things, before someone gets hurt.

May 9
Cincinnati

Pete Rose's Reds Alert came out today. Our seventh issue. And oh, hell. Bill Matthews has taken off after Darrel Chaney again. First it was Cesar Geronimo whom Matthews went after. Now Chaney. I'm in for it. I remember when Matthews started getting on Geronimo's case. I kept telling him not to do it.

One day he gets on Geronimo for a bad throw. The day before the article came out, Geronimo threw out two runners in one game. He throws out two, three guys and here's Matthews writing about a bad play he made a week ago.

He's on Geronimo, and at the time, Geronimo's hitting .300, our only .300 hitter. "How the hell can you be talking about how bad he is when he's the only .300 hitter we got?" I ask him.

But Matthews isn't listening. He believes statistics don't lie and he states Geronimo's statistics in the minor leagues, in the big leagues, with the Reds. He thinks he's an expert and he doesn't like Geronimo as a player.

"Hell," I say, "why don't you rip me or Bench? Bench is only hitting .150. But you gotta pick on Chaney."

Chaney's had troubles, true. But he isn't the reason we've been losing. Hell, he has a tough job, going in for defense in the late innings with the game on the line and with little chance to get the feel of things.

The story hurt me as much as it hurt Chaney. I mean, he's my teammate. I didn't want bad things written about Chaney.

Darrel was mad at first. So were a couple of other guys. But mostly they laughed about it, just like they do about all rips that show up in the paper.

And, believe me, no one in the clubhouse thought I had anything to do with it.

May 12
Cincinnati

I thought people might have learned from what happened to me in those National League playoffs. At least the people in Cincinnati. This is my home town. I'm proud of it. I was born here, grew up here, and spent my entire baseball career here.

And always the fans have been the greatest. I mean the absolute greatest. Sure, they boo. But that's part of the fun.

Today, though, I wasn't so proud. Now I know it wasn't everyone. But the few who took part in what I saw today put a smear on the entire population of Cincinnati.

Bob Watson, the Houston outfielder, ran into the wall in the second game of a doubleheader sweep for us. He hit his face against the wood and broke his glasses, cutting himself deeply.

He went down like he'd been shot, laying there on the warning track with blood pouring out of the gash. That wasn't the only thing pouring. Fans up in the second row right above him started pouring beer on him. Three glasses of beer in all were thrown. I mean, who knew how seriously he was hurt? Had glass gotten into his eye? Certainly the cut was ugly enough to suggest he was seriously hurt.

He was lying there, his teammates around him and Sparky Anderson out there to see if he could help, and the beer was coming down. "You sons-of-bitches," Sparky shouted, looking up at the crowd. "Get your ass down here," demanded Doug Rader, Houston's hot-tempered third baseman.

"Get your head down," ordered Sparky to Rader. "I don't want you getting hit with anything in my ball park."

Now Cesar Cedeno, the first man to reach Watson, was shouting at the fans. They were all long-haired, bearded. They were all drunk. They were shouting back at Cedeno.

"Shut up," commanded Sparky, now speaking to Cedeno. "Let me handle 'em. You're gonna be out here where they can throw things at you. I'll be in the dugout."

It took a while but peace finally was restored in left field. Watson was carted off to the hospital for twelve stitches. All this time I was thinking that the guys throwing beer better thank someone that they weren't down on the field where Rader, Lee May, and Cedeno could get their hands on them. They'd have torn them apart and it would have been justifiable homicide.

By then the security men were out in the trouble section. Our culprits, who I could see from the dugout, were sitting there like little angels. But they were not going to get away with this.

There are still decent people left in the world. All of a sudden, the other folks in the left-field stands were pointing out the guilty for the police. I loved that. It's the one way we can stop this at the ball park. The good people have to help.

Now the police were clearing the second row out. These guys were flat out smashed. A Sunday doubleheader in the sun, drinking beer, does strange things to people. One kid couldn't even get up. They had to carry him out.

Everything was lovely, except for outside. All they were going to do was eject the guilty from the park. I guess some other fans didn't think that was enough. They went out back and started fighting with the courageous beer throwers. A couple of people were arrested.

The Astros were mad after the game. Not only because they lost two games, but because of the incident.

"They talk about New York fans. That was the worst display of sportsmanship I've ever seen," said Don Wilson, a pitcher.

"They threw three beers and he was laying there bleeding. I wish I could have climbed up there with a ladder. There's something wrong with this town," added Cedeno.

Even my old teammate, Lee May, who knows the fans here, was damn mad. "That's the first time I've seen anything like that," May told me. "It surprised me. But, I guess you can't judge a whole crowd on a handful of idiots."

No, you certainly can't. But too many people do.

May 13
Cincinnati

Al Michaels was our play-by-play announcer for three years and not a bad dude.

Today the Giants are in town and San Francisco's where he's working now. He loves it, though, when he can get together with Joe Nuxhall, who was his color man.

Nux has just finished pitching batting practice, as he does almost every day for us. Michaels comes in the clubhouse and they start getting on each other.

"I made you what you are," says Nuxhall. "Taught you every damn thing you know."

"Are you kidding?" answers Michaels. "I carried you for three years."

They go back and forth as Nux sits there cooling off from the batting practice. Finally, Michaels looks at the huge man sitting in his locker sweating.

"You," he says to Nuxhall, "are the only announcer in the big leagues who keeps his job because of his arm instead of his voice."

Nuxhall couldn't answer that.

We had an answer for the Giants. His name was Don Gullett, and he combined with Pedro Borbon to win 4-1.

May 15
Cincinnati

Today a journalistic empire crumbled. Crushed to the ground by the heavy hand of management.

It started with a phone call from Dick Wagner, vice-president and hatchet man of the Reds.

"Pete," he says, "you don't have authorization to have your name on *The Reds Alert*. We'd like for you to take your name off the paper."

I was a little stunned, didn't answer at first. That was all Wagner needed.

"We can take legal action," he says. "You're going to take it off there."

71

"Hey, Dick," I said. "I'm worried about catching the Dodgers and playing ball. I don't want to be worried about going to court with you. Sure, I'll take my name off. If you want me to, I'll take it off."

Bob Howsam stated the Reds took action because of "a series of articles that have ridiculed and unfairly criticized various members of the Cincinnati team." The statement went on to say that the Reds didn't believe in censorship but that they didn't believe "it is right for a publication known as Pete Rose's paper to attack Rose's teammates, even though Pete has not personally authorized such articles."

It didn't exactly bother them when the paper printed 200 action photos or when it ran free full-page ads for the Reds in the first eight editions.

Matthews was fuming. "I very much deplore that honest, objective journalism has been termed 'ridicule' by the management of the Cincinnati Reds," he announced to the media. "This would appear to be a classic case of an effort to muzzle, however delicately, the efforts to report the day-to-day happenings of a major league baseball team as they actually happen."

To me, Bill merely said, "I just can't come out and say Pete Rose is gone."

I got on his tail about the articles and he wanted to fight it some. So, we arranged a meeting.

May 16
Cincinnati

It was meeting time: me, Dick Wagner, and the Reds' public relations director, Jim Ferguson, a former newspaperman who has become a house shill.

I went through the whole spiel about how I got my name

72

on the paper. It seems they got approval for the name *Reds Alert*, but they were so pressed for time when I entered the picture that they didn't go to get approval for *Pete Rose's Reds Alert*.

Wagner had a negative attitude going in. I wasn't going to get anywhere. "Damn, Dick, you think they aren't hurting me when they write bad about my players?" I said.

"Sure I do," he answered. "But people who pick that paper up will think you wrote the articles."

I disagree. I don't think anybody who reads an article that carries the name, "Full Count by Bill Matthews" is going to think I wrote it.

Now understand this. Every edition of the paper carried this disclaimer: "*Pete Rose's Reds Alert* is not a publication of the Cincinnati Reds Professional Baseball Team," and it said I was responsible only for what ran as my column.

"People don't read that," said Wagner. "They only know it's your magazine and think you're writing about your players."

That is just how this man thinks of the public, too. Doesn't give them much credit. He added he was worried about the bad publicity and, even more important, about hard feelings among the players.

There were no hard feelings. Quite the contrary. Chaney was really upset when he learned I was going to lose the paper. He thought it would cost me money, and, worse yet, hurt the two kids running the paper. "I really like them," he said.

If the front office would just get down to the locker room and sit around and chew the fat with the guys and get to know the life, they might realize what the hell's going on. I've been trying to tell Howsam this for years.

But it's over. I am out of the newspaper business. Well, not completely out yet. But I will be October 1.

For the second night in a row, I got two singles in five tries tonight as we beat Houston for the second straight time. But don't call me a singles hitter. Oh, I know last year I hit 181 singles, which is more than any switch-hitter in history. But I don't look at myself as a singles hitter.

I'm not a home-run threat, but you can't play me in. You have to play back when I'm hitting and that really helps. The bloops I hit will drop in, but the outfielders have to be deep enough to protect against the extra-base hit in the gap.

A guy like me is important to a team. Take the greatest home-run hitter in the world; if he gets 45 homers and there's nobody on base, all he has is 45 runs batted in. But guys like me or Ralph Garr, Felix Millan, Dave Cash, or Rod Carew, we set the table. I know the guys behind me hope I have a good year because that makes them more valuable.

I'm a little different from a lot of lead-off hitters. I look for a pitch to hit hard and it doesn't have to be a strike. I'm not a drastic bad-ball hitter, but I have my own strike zone. If I lay off every close pitch, it will take away my aggressiveness and that's the one thing I can't lose. I'd never get a hit.

Ralph Garr's the same with Atlanta. He's like Clemente. If he can reach it, he swings at it. It's just a good thing that no one tried to teach him the strike zone. He wouldn't be leading the world in base hits now if they did.

What the hell's going on here? You'd think I'd just come and told the people of Los Angeles that their most famous landmark—Raquel Welch—is a female impersonator.

I come out on the field and they're booing me and cussing me and throwing things at me like I'm some kind of villain.

Sure, I had that fight with Harrelson last year, but that was last year and that was in New York. Don't these people ever forget?

I wasn't ready for this. Oh, I figured I'd get booed. I helped beat the Dodgers out of the Western Division championship last year. But this is about the worst I've ever seen, except for the scene in Shea Stadium last year.

And dirty? Even I can't believe it. These people in the bleachers are sick. And they're getting a little personal, stuff about my mother and the like. The owners have to be worried about this. There are women and children up there. Not twenty feet away from a guy who's shouting obscenities at me is a man and his wife or girl. I think I'd have to get myself punched if I was in the stands. I'd be damned if I'd let anyone shout words like that if I were there with my wife and kids.

Okay, a ticket gives a fan a right to yell and scream, but you can go too far. We are human beings out there. We hear what is said.

Just to make matters worse, we lose a game we have to win. It's starting to look like the Dodgers are the team to beat and they knock us off, 5-4, with Jimmy Wynn hitting two home runs.

And the fans are throwing things at me. Bottles, apples, golf balls, things that can really hurt. It gets so bad that the Dodgers finally turn to their message board and, for the first time since they've been in L.A., put up a message to try to calm down the fans. It doesn't work.

I've been through quite a few bombardments from the stands in my eleven years in the big leagues. I've never really learned to understand them.

I remember one in Philadelphia. We were at bat when

some jokers in the upper deck at Veterans Stadium started hurling flashlight batteries down at the players. Imagine. One of those things hurled out of the upper deck and hitting a man on the top of his head could be lethal. You couldn't condemn everyone because of a few jerks, but it seems to me that that incident should have been policed by the fans themselves. They should have stopped the guy as soon as they saw him letting loose. It got so bad the umpire at first base figured he needed some protection. He got a Cincinnati batting helmet. Now that took a lot of nerve, to umpire a game in Philadelphia while wearing a Reds' helmet. But that's how bad it was.

The battery bombardment was nothing, though, compared to what happened one night in Los Angeles. We were playing a routine game against the Dodgers. I was in left field when all of a sudden, out of nowhere, there was this explosion. It sounded like a firecracker. I looked around and didn't see anything. Then I gazed toward the infield, and at shortstop there was this white powder scattered all over the ground. As white as the powder was Woody Woodward, our shortstop. He was totally shaken and well he should have been. Someone, as far as I know still unknown to this day, had flown over Dodger Stadium in a private plane. When he was directly overhead, it was bombs away. He dumped a 25-pound sack of flour out of the plane.

That has to be one of the most amazing displays of nerve ever. The guy has got to be a bank robber by profession. Twenty-five pounds of flour dropped from a plane could kill someone and might have killed Woodward had no one been on base. Woody just happened to be lucky. A runner was on second and he had moved in behind the runner when the flour hit. The sack landed just about in the spot Woodward would have been occupying with no one on base.

The incidents just go on and on. A few years back, I found myself in the midst of an angry mob in Chicago, not that that's so unusual, since I'm always the center of attention there. The Bleacher Bums and I have this thing going. They're always taunting me.

During batting practice I go out to the outfield and throw them up a baseball. Anywhere else, a fan would love to get a ball. Not in Chicago. As soon as that ball gets up in the bleachers, they start chanting, "Throw it back, throw it back." Whoever gets the ball throws it back. Twenty times I'll try to give away a baseball and it always comes back.

Then they'll start singing. "Rose is a fairy. Rose is a fairy." On and on it goes. It's all in good fun. I mean I like the Bleacher Bums. I have fun with them. One day they threw a crutch down on the field for me during a nationally televised game. I guess the guy who threw it went home with one crutch. Or maybe he's still there, waiting for his leg to heal.

The Bleacher Bums are bigger hams than the fans in New York. They like that television exposure and the national attention. They're more into it than the New York fans. They go to every game and are organized into a group. They have cheerleaders and singing groups.

In fact, I met a couple of them. They presented me with an honorary Bleacher Bum membership and I carry the card in my billfold. That's what I call being organized.

My Chicago notoriety, if I dare call it that, started with a freak thing, too, just like in New York. I laid down a bunt I thought I could beat out. I was going full speed and, just as I got near first base, made a long final stride toward the bag.

Ernie Banks was playing first base and his foot was directly over the base. I stepped on his ankle. By the time I saw it, I couldn't change without breaking a leg. The replay showed his foot directly in the middle of the base, but Banks is like a God in Chicago and all the fans, 35,000 of them that day, thought I was trying to hurt their star—and the only way they could let me know was to boo.

That got it started. It reached its climax the next year. All I did was ruin the fans' beloved Cubs by going 12-for-18 in a four-game series. That they didn't like too much and they became so rowdy I needed three policemen to escort me from Wrigley Field.

It was a good thing the police were there, too. One guy sneaked up behind me with one of those little souvenir bats and was about to club me in the head when Bob Lee, one of our pitchers and maybe the biggest man this side of Ted Kluszewski, almost punched his head off. That clubbing would have smarted.

It got worse, though. One woman reached out and socked me with her umbrella. A policeman decked her. Imagine, a woman hitting me with an umbrella because I did what I'm supposed to do and got twelve hits in the series.

May 21
Los Angeles

Sparky Anderson decided he'd try to calm down the fans in the left-field bleachers tonight. We're holding batting practice before the game and Sparky wanders out to left field. Before you know it, he's out there talking to the people. He knows it isn't everyone who's doing the throwing and shouting the obscenities. It's mostly kids.

A little old lady—she has to be 70—finally gets Sparky's ear. "I hope you realize it isn't all of us," she says.

"Sure I do," answers Sparky.

"I'm the head of the Jimmy Wynn Fan Club. We love him," she adds.

"He's a great player," says Sparky as diplomatically as possible.

"You know, you won't catch our Dodgers this year," the woman adds.

"Not if you keep playing .750 ball," answers Sparky.

He gets a promise of peace. It ends up being one of the shortest treaties of all time. They break it in the first inning. I'm going out of my mind. Really, I can't concentrate. Every time there's a fly ball, I figure something's going to hit me right in the head.

Last night, for example, Bill Russell hit a fly ball to me. I got under it, was just about to catch it, and this big chunk of ice went whizzing by my ear. I could hear it, that's how close it was. If it hit me in the eye, it could be my career.

Concentration doesn't come easy. I go 0-for-4 again. Morgan hits his second homer in two nights, but it doesn't help as Joe Ferguson hits a sacrifice fly to score Willie Crawford in the bottom of the ninth inning and the Dodgers win again, 3-2.

May 22
Los Angeles

Goodbye, Los Angeles. May you choke in your own smog.

I didn't think I'd ever make this statement, but for the first time in my career, baseball wasn't any fun. That's how bad they worked me over out here.

Usually I react to the boos and the crowd. It drives me to play even harder. But this was too much. I couldn't concentrate. It was just awful. Even in the playoffs against New York I had fun, but this wasn't fun. It was torture.

I didn't get a hit in the whole damn series. An important series like this and we lose three games and I go 0-for-13. It just can't be.

79

Never had I thought like this before. I was walking up to the plate and all that was running through my mind was, "Let me hit and get it over with in a hurry. I just want to get out of this city."

Sparky had to have a talk with me before the last game, the one we lost, 6-3.

"Now just calm down and forget about the fans as best you can," he told me. But have you ever tried to forget about the fans when they're throwing everything under the sun at you and cussing you as though you were some kind of sub-human species?

This was the worst I'd ever seen. There were fights breaking out everywhere all night. What a crowd! And me . . . I'm 0-for-19. That's the worst slump of my career. Three times before, I was 0-for-18. But 0-for-19, never.

May 24
San Diego

Herman Levy is a legend in his own time and if you haven't heard of him, you haven't spent time in the visitors' clubhouse in San Diego Stadium.

And I mean it just that way. Spent time. Herman tries harder than any other human being on earth to do his job right. He's just one of those guys who disaster naturally follows.

Today, for example, Herman decided to clean the mustard jar. So, quite naturally, the first thing he did was empty out the mustard. He emptied it into this big pot, then shoved the pot in the freezer.

Cleaned the hell out of the jar. Now came time to put the mustard back in the jar and . . . well, did you ever see a huge chunk of frozen mustard?

Nothing particularly unusual for Herman Levy, 66, son of a street sweeper on the Lower East Side of Manhattan.

80

Believe it or not, I saw Herman spend half an hour one day looking for "the key to the batter's box."

Last year, just before heading out to the bullpen, Jack Billingham, one of our pitchers, told him that he gets hungry during the game.

"How about sending out a ham sandwich on rye in the fifth inning," said Billingham.

"Sure," said Herman.

By the fifth inning, Billingham had forgotten all about this little joke. Anyone knows a Cincinnati player isn't allowed to sit in the bullpen with a ham sandwich.

Out of the clubhouse came the bat boy, carrying the sandwich. To get to the bullpen, he had to go through the dugout, and to go through the dugout, he had to go past Sparky Anderson. Anderson saw the bat boy.

"Whatcha got there?" he asked.

"A ham sandwich for Mr. Billingham," answered the kid.

"Give me that," Sparky fumed, grabbing the sandwich and carefully smashing it into a little ball.

"Here, give this to Mr. Billingham and tell him I don't think it looks very good for a $50 sandwich," shouted Sparky.

The fine, of course, was removed when Sparky learned it was just supposed to be another joke on Herman.

Herman Levy is always trying to do something nice for somebody. One night the Atlanta Braves were in town and Herman was going to give them special treatment. He went out and bought 35 individual enchilada dinners.

During the seventh inning, he put them into the oven to get them warm. In the ninth, the hungry players came strolling in from the field for their treat.

Herman went over and what he found was 35 individual enchilada dinners floating in melted cellophane. He forgot to unwrap them.

This spring, though, Herman may have outdone himself.

It was raining in Phoenix, where the Padres were supposed to play a game. Some of the Padre players were looking for a movie.

"Hey, Herman, do you know where there's a movie within walking distance?" they asked.

"Sure," said Herman. "About eight blocks down the street."

"Are you certain?" they pressed.

"Sure, I'm certain," he answered.

So off they went in mid-afternoon, walking eight blocks to Herman's movie theater.

It wasn't long before they returned looking for Herman.

"What's wrong?" he said.

"There was a theater there, all right. A drive-in theater," they told him.

May 25
San Diego

Yogi Berra, so the story goes, hadn't had a hit in quite some time when a reporter asked him to explain his slump.

"Slump?" Yogi answered. "I ain't in no slump. I just ain't hitting."

Well, Yogi baby, I got news for you. I'm in a slump. And tonight it reached the point of being ridiculous. Seems like only yesterday I was hitting .309. Today I'm at .259 and that's a drop of 50 points.

It reached its low point tonight. Even Jack Billingham, who has to be the worst hitter in all of baseball, got his first hit of the year. We got 13 hits and won, 12-4.

Me? I was 0-for-2 with four walks. And it was so humiliating.

I mean here we were in the eighth inning. Mike McQueen, who was out all of last season with a broken hip, and I were standing in the on-deck circle.

"What kind of hitter are you?" I asked Mike.

"Don't rightly know," he drawled. "I ain't swung a bat in two years."

Sure enough. First pitch. A single. Me? I bounced out.

So after the game I'm taking it real good. McQueen's standing there giving me some tips. I'm 0-for-my-last-7 again and I need tips.

"We'd better guard the pool tonight," laughs Morgan in the clubhouse. "Pete might just jump out of his window into it. We'll find him floating, face down, in the morning."

"Don't worry about that," answered Ted Kluszewski. "He won't hit that, either."

Ha, ha!

Hits just won't come. When you're going like this, it looks like even the umpires have gloves.

May 26
San Diego

I've got to come out of it.

Well, they didn't find Pete Rose lying face down in the swimming pool this morning. Almost, but not quite.

I just kept after them and today things happened right. Not that the day began too well. My first time up I hit the ball hard—right at the left fielder.

"Oh, no, not this again," I thought.

But my next time up, with Cesar Geronimo on second base, it happened. Another line drive, this one off the right-field wall about a foot from the top, almost a home run. Instead, I got a single as Bobby Tolan played it perfectly and got it into second base. I hit the damn ball so hard that he could handle it and keep me to a single. Oh, well, it was a hit.

Before the game was over, with us winning, 4-1, I got another hit. Tomorrow, home and the Mets. I wonder how the fans will treat Harrelson. Hope they treat him better than I've been treated. I mean, the Mets are going lousy and I'd hate to wake them up.

May 28
Cincinnati

Tonight I almost killed myself. Really. It was the seventh inning against the New York Mets, two out, none on and the Reds in front, 7-2.

Worse yet, it came on a foul ball, so it was almost a meaningless play—except that I don't believe there is such a thing in this game. You go all out all the time. You owe that to your teammates, to the fans, and most of all, to yourself.

Dave Schenck sent a soft fly down the left-field line. I came over and I was flying, literally. Just as I crossed the foul line, I reached out backhanded and grabbed the ball about knee high.

All of a sudden everything went crazy. I was flying through the air and, to be honest, I couldn't tell you what happened at that exact moment.

Later I watched the replay. Jeez. I stepped on the bullpen mound in foul territory, tripped and crashed headlong into the fence. Somehow, too, I held the ball for the final out. It was the final out of the game for me, too. The arm started swelling immediately.

If I do say so myself, it was a helluva catch, the kind I'm proud of because I made the play out of sheer hustle, managed to survive a battle with the wall, and held on to the ball.

Was this the best catch I ever made? Probably not. It was Willie Mays who said, "I don't rank 'em, I just catch 'em." I'm not sure I can name the best catch I made.

84

There have been a lot of good ones. I run into a lot of walls, usually at an angle so I don't get hurt. And I play extremely shallow for a left fielder, so I make a lot of catches running away from the plate.

In the 1972 playoffs, I made a diving catch in left center off Pirate pitcher Dave Giusti that has to rank somewhere near the top. The AstroTurf was wet and I slid a long way to catch that one. The game, too, was rather important.

I guess, though, if one catch stands out, it is one I made in 1969 in Atlanta. This wasn't exactly what you'd call a spectacular play. Just unusual. And what followed it was funny as hell.

Alex Johnson is in left field on this day and I'm in center. Now Alex plays left field about as well as I play chess. And I don't play at all. Anyway, someone hits one that sure as hell is a home run. A.J.—that's Alex Johnson—goes back to the wall, leaps up, and slaps at the ball, just trying to knock it back into play.

Sure enough, he gets the ball in the web of his glove, it goes straight up into the air and comes down. I'm standing there and catch it. Now, don't ask me what I'm doing in straightaway left field on a ball that looks like a home run. I just hustled over there out of instinct and out of knowing what kind of fielder A.J. is.

It goes as a 7-8 put-out if you're keeping score, and that's a play you don't see every day.

But the best part is yet to come. I'll be damned if two innings later, bases loaded, the game on the line, Sonny Jackson doesn't hit a line drive right at A.J.

You know Alex, ole clank. The ball hits right in his glove, waist high, and he drops it.

He looks down at the ball lying at his feet, the winning run crossing the plate. Then he looks at me and shouts: "Where were you?"

I picked up the newspaper this morning and couldn't believe what I saw. Sparky was being quoted as saying I'd probably miss a couple of games with my injured arm.

Four years and Sparky doesn't know me better than that. Yeah, the arm hurts and it's swollen and discolored. But that isn't going to keep me out of the lineup.

When I hit that damn wall last night, I thought the wrist was broken. The first thing I did was move it to see that it wasn't. As soon as it moved, I knew I'd be playing tonight.

I guess there were a few other people who knew it, too. Sparky came to me before the game. "You okay?" he asked.

"Sure," I answered.

"Okay, you're playing. I knew I couldn't get you out of there. Even my butcher knew it. I went to him this morning for some meat and he says to me, 'Don't worry, he'll play.' That's when I knew for sure. If the butcher says so, it has to be."

Come to think of it, I couldn't sit out if the arm were broken. Perez and Morgan would ride me so heavy that I couldn't take it. You don't sit out when Jon Matlack's pitching for the Mets.

I went into the training room to get our little trainer, Larry Starr, to look at the arm.

"Phew," he said, "no telling what might have happened if it had been anyone but you hitting that wall. You caught the wall just right. If you'd hit with your collarbone, it would have broken for sure."

I should only hurt so much every night. I got two hits, a single, and a double off Matlack. Perez won it in the tenth with a home run off my old friend, Harry Parker, of playoff fame.

The Biltmore Hotel is at 43rd Street and Madison Avenue. It's an old hotel, filled with memories of F. Scott Fitzgerald and his gang. I know about him because of all the publicity the movie "The Great Gatsby" is getting.

It's 5:15 in the afternoon. The streets of New York are alive with the rush-hour traffic and there is a crowd gathering around our bus.

I'm sitting by the window and I'm the one they want to see. This, you see, is the day I return to Shea Stadium for the first time since last October's playoff and fight.

This crowd isn't hostile. They want autographs and most of them are familiar, the same group of autograph hounds that always hang around the Biltmore.

Two kids unveil a sign. "Rose Is a Bum," it says. I've got to laugh. Right there in downtown Manhattan in the middle of rush hour there's a sign that says, "Rose Is a Bum."

I put my autograph on the sign. Really, I'm not scared about tonight, no matter what happened in the past.

I've got the *New York Post* in front of me on the bus. I see that Harrelson is trying to quiet things down before they get started.

"I'm hopeful our fans won't do anything, so they can prove they are good fans," Bud told this reporter. "Pete and I are tired of the whole thing and if people would stop writing about it the nuts would stop coming out to the parks."

We arrive at Shea and, as usual, there are hundreds of kids hanging around waiting for autographs. Now they've got people on hand to guard me but I stop to sign. What the hell, I'm going to be out there in front of them in an hour. I might as well make some friends right now.

We dress and head for the field. I can't escape it. They want to know how I feel.

"Every time a plane goes over I'm gonna be ducking," I laugh.

Sparky Anderson comes up to me.

"Look," he says to me, "it's half the Mets' responsibility to keep peace, but it's half ours. The best thing for us to do is go out and keep our mouths shut. If anyone calls us a bad name, we have to just pretend they said, 'hello there.' "

It will be a pleasure.

Joe Reichler, the assistant to the baseball commissioner, is on hand. He says he's here to give me an All-Star ring that I lost. Could be. But he's also here in case there's a riot and some decision has to be made. If it's that important, where the hell is the commissioner?

"You knew what you were doing four years ago when you sent me to Vietnam to get ready for this," I tell Reichler, thinking of the goodwill journey I took to Vietnam with Joe DiMaggio.

I walk out on the field, and as soon as they see me they start in. You can't hear yourself think with the jets roaring into LaGuardia Airport overhead and the boos from the crowd.

One thing stands out. The left-field stands are empty. Only policemen stand there. I've got myself three plain-clothesmen and there are 25 extra cops on hand.

I wonder if Brezhnev had as much security?

A kid in the front is yelling at me.

"Get a haircut," I shout at him.

He laughs.

I only notice one sign: "Rose, We'll Never Forget."

I go through batting practice, trying to keep to myself, away from the reporters and the crowd. I have a baseball game to play.

They begin the starting lineups. "Leading off for Cincinnati and playing left field. . . ."

That's all I can hear. The boos come louder and louder.

I walk into the batter's box to start the game. Jon Matlack, as fine a young left-hander as there is in the league, is pitching. He throws. Base hit, first pitch.

That meant something extra to me. Getting a hit off Matlack any time is an accomplishment, but getting one under these circumstances, well, it showed that I was concentrating.

It was to be my only hit of the game but not the only thing I did. I have to admit it, I was juiced up. In fact, I knew I would be all series. But I was happy, too. We won, 5-2, behind Clay Kirby. Nothing happened that could be termed fan reaction. They booed but they didn't shout obscenities. They didn't throw things.

Hell, I wish these New York fans had been in Los Angeles.

June 4
New York

They let a few fans wander into the left-field seats today and again it was calm. Oh, I had a whiskey bottle thrown at me while I was hitting, but it didn't come close enough to worry me.

It took us a while to win this one—our tenth win in the last eleven games. We went ten innings and won it, 6-3.

Sparky played one of his hunches today. He let Danny Driessen hit in the game-winning situation; Driessen had gone sixteen straight times to the plate without a hit. The hunch, like all of Sparky's, paid off and Driessen wound up tying the game for us. His hit was off my old buddy Harry Parker. Harry's got to be wondering what the hell's going on every time he comes in against the Reds.

I have to admit that I had the fans buzzing twice today. Both times—in the third and eighth innings—I hit routine double-play balls. Except there was no way anyone on earth was going to double me. Not in New York. Not in front of those fans. I ran like I never ran before and beat both plays. It was Charlie Hustle at his best.

If *Sport Magazine* had planned it, they couldn't have come up with better timing. An off-day in New York and, as a promotion for an upcoming issue with me on the cover, they held a luncheon with the guests of honor being me and—who else?—Bud Harrelson.

The newspaper, radio, and TV guys turned out in full force. Like everyone else, they like a free meal. But the turnout was increased no small amount the night before when the Cleveland Indians and the Texas Rangers wound up battling with the fans.

It was a ten-cent beer night in Cleveland. And, a week back the two teams got into a brawl in Arlington, Texas. That sparked it. There's no way that fight would have happened last night if they didn't have the earlier one.

It must have been something. The newspaper pictures I saw showed the fans out there attacking the players. Probably worse than what happened to us in the playoffs.

The world is nutty. Something has to be done before a player gets hurt. But you can't build fences. This is an outdoor sport, not a concentration camp.

Bud's pretty much of the same mind. He thinks the clubs have to get tougher with the customers. "If I'd been running the show during the playoffs, I'd have had guards down both foul lines, armed with clubs and ready to start swinging," said Bud.

And I'm the villain?

90

I can hit Tom Seaver. I know it and he knows it. It's as simple as that.

He's a power pitcher, the kind who challenges the hitter. I like that. He's a control pitcher. He knows where the baseball is going. I like that.

It all adds up to the fact that Seaver will challenge me with fast balls and they will be strikes. Also, I'll get my cuts at him.

Today I faced him four times and got three hits. I hit a single and scored a run. I hit a triple, drove in a run, and scored later. I hit a double.

Still, that left us tied, 3-3, going into the ninth. With Joe Morgan at second and Ray Sadecki pitching, I hit my hardest ball of the game. A line drive to deepest center. It was an out.

Had that been anywhere else it would have won the game. As it was, a long homer by John Milner off Pedro Borbon gave the Mets their fourth run and they beat us, 4-3.

Oh well, it was just the kind of series I was hoping to have on my return to Shea Stadium, 6-for-13 and two wins in three games. And, no violence.

But it ended on a note that was a reminder of the problem that might have existed. Before I went out to my position in the ninth inning, a groundskeeper came up to me.

"The head of security wants you to run through the bullpen and under the stands as soon as the third out is made. He says you've gotten through safely so far and he doesn't want to take any chance."

I did as directed. Kind of scarey, isn't it?

Haven't things changed here! This is the town where they used to boo the kids who couldn't find the eggs in an Easter egg hunt.

Philadelphia was always something unique. A born loser.

But don't look now. The Phils are challenging for the Eastern Division championship. They are in first place and the town is going wild. The fans are pouring into the new ball park and they are coming to cheer their heroes, not boo them. What will they think of next?

Today, though, wasn't exactly the happiest of days for Philadelphia fans. It was announced just before game time that Greg Luzinski, the powerful young outfielder, will have knee surgery and be out probably for the rest of the season.

That is a tough break. I like Luzinski. He's going to be a tremendous player, if only because the ball park is perfectly made for him. Baseballs just fly out of Veterans Stadium and he's about the strongest thing going in the game today.

He's a dedicated player, too. And he took a lot of abuse in this town. The press isn't exactly the friendliest on earth. Last year when we came in, Luzinski was having a hell of a season and they ran a cartoon that showed him as being ridiculously fat.

Hell, he can't help it. He's just built big. And he can run.

But the Phils are going to have to make do without him and that will hurt. Now they don't have the power hitter to go behind Mike Schmidt.

Schmidt's having what you'd call a pleasant season. Some kind of power. He's been a big plus for the Phils.

I guess the biggest change they made was getting Dave Cash from Pittsburgh to play second base. Now they finally are both defensively and offensively strong up the middle, teaming Cash with Bowa, and that will help them.

Nothing helped the Phils much tonight, though. We gave Dick Baney, just back from Indianapolis, a start in place of Roger Nelson, and he held the Phils down long enough for us to go to work.

In the sixth Perez hit a two-run homer. We added two in the seventh and three in the ninth and won, 7-4.

June 8
Philadelphia

Every time I walk into Veterans Stadium I'm reminded of the two funniest lines I ever heard in baseball.

Both of them were uttered right here in this locker room. The first belonged to the inimitable Alex Johnson. Now A.J. didn't exactly like reporters. He also wasn't a man of many words.

We were at old Connie Mack Stadium and Alex had just hit his ninth home run of the season. While A.J. is as strong as anyone in the game, he doesn't hit many home runs, being a line-drive hitter. The season before he had hit only four.

A reporter approached Alex and said: "Last year you only hit four homers and this year you've got nine already. What's the difference?"

Alex looked down at his feet, thought for a moment and then answered: "Five."

"I'm surprised he didn't say four," commented Tommy Helms when he heard that statement.

The other line came from Al Ferarra, one of the true characters of baseball. I mean anyone who says, "I wanted to be a big league baseball player so I could see my picture on a bubble gum card" has got to be funny.

Well, we'd just gotten Ferarra from San Diego in

exchange for a little-used outfielder named Angel Bravo. Ferarra was out patrolling left field on this afternoon and wound up making two spectacular catches on routine fly balls. One he had to dive for, the other he got backhand. Both times he should have been standing underneath waiting.

"You really made it exciting out there today, didn't you?" commented a reporter.

Ferarra looked at the guy. "What'd you expect for Angel Bravo, Willie Mays?"

I bring the two lines up only to try and get some humor in a humorless day. Dave Cash hit a double off Clay Carroll in the bottom of the ninth inning to score Tommy Hutton and we lost, 6-5.

It was a game we couldn't lose. Not when Bill Plummer hits two home runs off Steve Carlton and Bench hits one. But lose we did, and one of the big plays was an error by Clay Kirby, the pitcher we got from San Diego for Bobby Tolan.

Come to think of it, what'd we expect for Bobby Tolan, Bob Gibson?

June 9
Montreal

It's a good thing I make $160,000 a year playing baseball. If I didn't I might starve.

I don't usually go out much at night. It's a hassle with people recognizing you and the lot. So, I order room service. Usually I order breakfast and sometimes my late meal, say at 3:00 in the afternoon before going to the ball park.

A couple of weeks back, when we were in Los Angeles, I ordered up a couple of eggs, sausage, juice, and tea. It came to about $4. Not bad.

Then, the other day in New York, I ordered the same breakfast. They nailed me for $8.50.

Tonight after flying into Montreal from Philadelphia, I was hungry.

Here in Montreal they rob you with class. You pick up the phone and dial room service and the voice on the other end says, "Bonjour, service de chambre."

That's what I heard when I called for dinner for me and Phil Gagliano. We were in the middle of a gin game and ordered two steaks, two salads, and two iced teas.

That came to just $28. A bargain.

At least it seems to be a bargain compared to what happened to Dick Baney in New York. Baney had just joined the club, having spent the first part of the season with Indianapolis.

Baney ordered two cheeseburgers at the Biltmore. That's just what he got, two cheeseburgers.

"No onion, no pickle, no tomato. Not even hamburger buns. Just white bread," he told me.

Oh yes. The bill for two cheeseburgers? Only $15.

Baney couldn't believe it.

Food, however, isn't the only area where hotels take your money. Bucky Albers, a writer for the Dayton *Journal-Herald* who travels with us, found that out.

We were in Pittsburgh and Bucky needed a haircut. He went into the hotel barber shop and let the man carve away with the razor. A fine styling job. And cheap at the price.

"Eighteen dollars," screamed Albers for the rest of the trip. "Robbery."

Had Bucky learned his lesson? No sir.

He decided he needed some clean clothes in New York, so he sent a suit, two sets of underwear, and two pair of slacks to the hotel laundry.

The cleaning bill was $18.

Maybe I am underpaid.

If we keep playing like we did this afternoon, though, they'll have to be giving me more money. We got to the Phils for seven runs in the seventh inning—I walked and singled and Bench homered—another run in the eighth, and three more in the ninth, two of them on my single and Morgan's homer.

The result was a 14-7 win for Don Gullett and that makes up some for last night.

June 10
Montreal

Ron Fairly plays for the Montreal Expos and is a pretty good hitter. He also is a helluva guy.

Anyway, we started talking about the home run Mike Schmidt of the Phillies hit in the Astrodome the other night, the one that hit the speakers up on the roof and that would have hit the American flag in center if it had been able to keep going.

"I hit one that far once," said Fairly.

"Yeah?"

"I did. And I still bogeyed the hole."

Fairly didn't hit them too far tonight. But then we didn't hit them at all. Geronimo hit a home run, I had a single, and we lost 3-1 when the game was rained out in the ninth.

And what rain. I haven't seen anything like it in some time. I'll tell you how bad it was. Joe Nuxhall was up there in the press box, broadcasting the game. You remember Joe. Thirty years ago he broke into the big leagues at age 15, youngest player ever.

He pitched in a game and got two men out, was sent to the minors, returned to high school, and waited nine years before he came back to the big leagues and got the third out.

Anyway, Nux is up there telling stories when the rain really starts, and it's flowing into his broadcast booth. All of a sudden he's under water.

"And now, back to the station," he says as he's backing

away from the window. Just as he says it, boom, the window blows in and there is water everywhere. It wasn't any wonder the game was called off in the ninth.

Oh, yes, one other thing happened. In the eighth inning I walked and Morgan hit one that had to be a home run. He really belted it.

Ken Singleton, who was celebrating his 26th birthday, went back to the wall, jumped up, reached over the fence, and caught it.

Morgan couldn't believe it. He stood there at first base, hands thrown up in the air in disgust.

"Why does it always happen to me?" he asked.

Every ballplayer, when he gets robbed, thinks he's the only man on earth it ever happened to.

June 11
Montreal

Fairly was at it again. Another story. It takes place back in the days when he was with the Dodgers and Don Drysdale was pitching.

The Dodgers had a shortstop in those days named Bob Lillis, playing behind PeeWee Reese. That meant it had been seven Sundays since he started a game.

Anyway, on this one day everything goes wrong for Drysdale. The first guy walks, the next guy gets on with an error, there's a passed ball, a hit batter, the works. The other team scores three times and hasn't hit the ball out of the infield.

Drysdale comes steaming into the dugout. He reaches into the bat rack and grabs a bat, beginning at once to slam it against anything in sight. Slowly but surely the bat begins falling apart, a piece of it coming up and hitting Drysdale in the eye and causing a cut.

So here's Drysdale, splintered bat in his hand and his eye bleeding and mad as hell, and Lillis walks up to him.

"Don," Lillis says, "I really don't mind your using my bat, but that was my gamer."

That broke everyone up, even Drysdale.

Every player has a "gamer," the bat he uses in the game.

Let me tell you it's hard to get a good bat. The bat I use is 35 inches long and weighs 34 or 35 ounces.

There isn't much equipment that's more important to me than my bat. I take a bat out and, if it feels good to me, there's a load taken off my shoulders.

Used to be I'd order a dozen bats from Louisville Slugger. I don't do that any more. Out of a dozen there'd be maybe two that were what I was looking for.

So I went to Rex Bradley of Hillerich and Bradsby and said, "Look, send me whatever you can. I appreciate a wide grain. If it's only two or three bats, send them. I'd rather have two or three good ones than a dozen no good."

I figure there's no sense in the club's paying for bad bats.

I'm different from a lot of players. They don't like to use their game bats in batting practice. But if I get a good bat I use it in batting practice. I firmly believe that if I hit the ball well in practice, I'll hit well in the game. I like to go up there in BP and feel just like I do in a game.

I'm picky about my bats. I like the wide grain. Again, not everyone agrees. Ted Kluszewski, our batting coach, likes a narrow grain. The whole thing about a bat to me is the grain.

Morgan uses the narrow grain and a smaller bat. But it's the damnedest thing. Every time he gets a good bat it starts splitting down at the end.

Last year, when he went on a home-run spree, he was using a bat that was falling apart. He kept using it. It was just chipping away and he wouldn't give it up. I couldn't believe it. I've never seen a guy use a bat that's chipped like that one was.

Oh, yes, speaking of bats. Guess what happened to us tonight. We led the Expos, 5-1, going into the seventh inning. Then we gave them seven in the seventh and eight in the eighth.

We lost, 16-6, with Willie Davis driving in seven runs and hitting two homers, one with the bases loaded.

The Big Red Machine just can't get untracked.

June 12
Montreal

I found out today that Sparky didn't particularly like the way we lost yesterday, all those runs in the seventh and eighth innings.

Fact is, he was mad. So mad that he held a little meeting and threatened to hold a bed check on the pitchers.

Now the pitchers were mad.

"Why the hell doesn't he check everyone?" said one of the pitchers, and I kind of wondered, too. He'd never checked beds before, but then he never had any trouble on the club.

He doesn't allow drinking on the plane and everyone follows that rule, so there really isn't much of a problem.

And, he's the manager. He can do what he wants. I can't understand these guys playing baseball who say, "I can't play for that man."

I never had any trouble with a manager. I played for Fred Hutchinson, Dick Sisler, Don Hefner, Dave Bristol, and Sparky, and you'll never hear me say one bad word about any of them.

The only one I didn't hit .300 for was Hutch and he gave me the job. But I was Rookie of the Year for him.

The pitchers must have taken Sparky seriously. Kirby went out and pitched a seven-hitter and beat the Expos, 3-1.

Maybe that is the way to win this thing. Early to bed, early to rise, makes a man healthy, wealthy, and a pennant winner.

June 14
Cincinnati

Back home. We go against the Phillies and they are leading in the East.

Before the game I couldn't resist getting together with George Culver, one of their relief pitchers. Culver used to be a Red. In fact, he pitched a no-hitter when he was with us; it was against, of all people, the Phils.

Like so many other people in baseball, George has a rather colorful nickname—Skunk.

Take just our team if you want to know about nicknames. Tony Perez is The Big Dog, because he's the man we count on in the clutch. Cesar Geronimo is, quite naturally, Chief.

Danny Driessen, being in his first full season, is Rook, short for Rookie and a name he'll have trouble shaking. Darrel Chaney, our backup infielder, is Norton, and all you have to do is look at him to know why. He looks just like Art Carney as Ed Norton on Jackie Gleason's "Honeymooners."

A lot of guys pick up nicknames that are short for their real names. Hence, Phil Gagliano becomes Gags, Bill Plummer is Plum, and Terry Crowley, Crow.

Carroll, of course, is The Hawk and that comes from a face that belongs in a nest. Tommy Hall is The Blade and that refers to his physique. Roger Nelson is Spider, a takeoff on his weird pitching motion that makes him look like he has eight legs.

Baseball and nicknames go hand in hand. Alex Johnson, now with Texas but once with us, is A.J. Woody Woodward, once our shortstop but now our television color man, was Judy, a reference to his Punch and Judy style of hitting—one home run in his whole career.

Then there was Jim Maloney, who had a weird chest bone. He was always Tits, although that's a nickname that never seemed to get into print.

Even the manager can't escape. Sparky is Captain Hook, at least to his pitchers. They call him that because he's so quick to hook them out of a game.

And Bench calls him John McGraw. I think he likes that.

Anyway, I'm with Skunk and he's talking about how he's been with six teams, all of them winners, but he's still not getting his eight years in on the pension. "I've been running with Steve Carlton this year and that should count as two years on the pension," said Culver, and I got the message.

Just then Ron Schueler, who was to be the Phils' starting pitcher, walked up. "Well, I've been running with Carlton and Culver and I may not get four years in," he laughed.

He wasn't laughing much later. We knocked him out with six runs in the third inning and went on to win, 7-3.

I had a single, double, walk, and two runs batted in. It's good to be home.

June 15
Cincinnati

We lost tonight to the Phillies. The Dodgers had lost in the afternoon so we had a chance to gain a game, cut their lead to six, and make them start looking back over their shoulders at us. But we blew it, 5-2.

I went 0-for-4. Can't get it together. But at least tonight

101

it wasn't only me. Jim Lonborg pitched and he was super. We got only five hits and that should tell you something.

I kind of get a kick out of seeing Lonborg do so well. Remember him in 1967 when he won 22 games for the Boston Red Sox and won the Cy Young Award? He was just about the best pitcher in the game.

Then he broke his leg skiing at Lake Tahoe. Everyone gave up on him. He wound up back in the minors, trying to fight his way back. I guess it was Sparky who said it best. "Quality can come back," our manager said.

Lonborg is quality. He can't throw as hard as he once did, but he's a pitcher now, puts everything where he wants it and throws about four different pitches. He's got eight wins now and should be a top challenger for the Comeback of the Year Award.

Come to think of it, if I don't get unwound I may be going for that award next year.

June 16
Cincinnati

I was 0-for-5. When am I going to put it together?

Maybe never. What a slump this has been. And we keep winning. We beat the Phils, 5-0, behind Clay Carroll.

The Hawk had to come out of the bullpen and start because Roger Nelson's shoulder went south on him. He said he's had it before. Said he knows it isn't serious.

How come so many injuries are not serious, but the guy can't play?

Anyway, Hawk's on top of the world. He pitched eight shutout innings. You should have seen him, waiting at the door for the reporters.

"I ain't bragging, but when we get in a jam like this, it

seems they always call on me," he says. "I'm always the one."

Maybe he can bail me out. I mean my average is .271 and that hurts.

Oh, well, there's always tomorrow.

Tomorrow is here. Last night I sat around talking to my wife. What I told her was that I'm damn embarrassed.

I was lousy swinging the bat. I'm worrying about it too much. I don't know what it is. Maybe it's because I'm making so much. There aren't many people in the game making more than I am, and here I am at .271.

Maybe it's the MVP award. Maybe there's a jinx. I don't know.

What I do know is that for the past month, I've hit all of .263 and that isn't exactly overwhelming. Normally, I don't worry about slumps. A slump is a slump. But knowing how well I can hit makes this really amazing.

I'm coming out of it. Tonight. You can bet on it. I know I will because Sparky made the prediction I would and he isn't often wrong.

The Montreal Expos are the team we go against tonight and the game is on national television. That really juices me up. I just love it when I know millions of people are watching.

Anyway, Sparky was sitting with Tony Kubek, the former Yankee player, who now is a broadcaster.

"Pete'll come out of it tonight and go on a five-week spree when he hits .350," said Sparky.

Okay, Spark, I'll try to make you live up to it.

103

Batting practice is unreal. I hit the ball all over the lot and am I high. I can't wait for the damn game to start. All of a sudden, out of nowhere, I've got my stroke back.

"If I don't get three hits tonight, you can find me up on the suspension bridge, ready to jump," I told Morgan.

He laughed. He can laugh, the way he's swinging. He hit about eight out in batting practice.

"Oh, man, hitting's easy," he shouted.

Game time. First inning, single. That ends an 0-for-9 slump.

Second time up, walk. Dammit, why not throw it over? I've got it going.

Third time up, single, good for a run. Fourth time, single, again good for a run.

Finally a ground out. Three-for-four, two runs batted in, two runs scored.

Look out, Ralph Garr, I'm coming at you. I know you lead the league in hitting and you already have 100 hits. But here I come.

Just like last year. You remember, 52 hits in July and 47 in August. A .373 average from June 27 on.

I'm ready now.

June 18
Cincinnati

Gene Mauch manages the Montreal Expos and he is, depending on whether you like him or not, a genius or a bum. He's never won a pennant but he never is looking for work, either. He's one of those 24-hour-a-day men. He is always thinking baseball, trying to come up with some little edge.

I've always liked the way he managed, although they say in 1964 he blew the pennant for the Phillies by overworking

Jim Bunning and Chris Short down the stretch. I'm not sure he blew it. I'm not so sure his team was good enough to win it.

I do know he likes me. One time he said that, with my hustle, I epitomize what every big league team tries to teach in its minor league organization.

There was a time, though, when I hated the man. That was when I first came to the big leagues. Damn, he'd yell at me: "Get this hot dog. He can't hit nothing. You hear me, hot dog." He'd shout on and on. He did it with everyone, I guess. He yelled at Helms and he yelled at Tommy Harper. He'd always be yelling until you did well against him.

Back in 1966 I'm just hitting everything the Phils are throwing up there. I mean I'm murdering them. We're playing in old Connie Mack Stadium and I come to the plate for the first time.

"Pete," Mike Ryan, the catcher, says, "Gene told me to tell what pitch is coming."

I'll be damned. He starts telling me and it screws my mind up but good. The first three times up I can't hit the ball and I'm shouting at the umpire, "Tell him to shut up. I don't want to know what's coming."

We get down to the ninth inning, two out and a man on. I go up to bat and he tells me again. I say to myself, "This guy has been telling me all night what the pitch is. He ain't gonna stop now."

So he tells me a curve is coming and I hit that SOB off the scoreboard. The run scores and we win the game by one run.

Next night I come up to the plate and Ryan's catching again. "Pete," he says, "Gene told me to tell you to go to hell."

Well, I haven't stopped hitting against Gene Mauch's teams. I got a double tonight and it drove in a run. Trouble was, it was one of only two hits we could get off Ernie

McAnally. The Expos beat us, 2-1, when Jim Cox, a rookie second baseman, hit a ninth-inning home run off Clay Kirby.

Maybe we should start telling Cox what pitch is coming, huh, Gene?

June 19
Cincinnati

I ran into Greg Cook in downtown Cincinnati today. You might remember Greg. He was Rookie of the Year in the National Football League a few years back.

He might have been one of the greatest quarterbacks of all time if he hadn't busted up his shoulder. He's been trying to come back for the past three years, but hasn't been able to make it.

We got to talking football and the Cincinnati Bengals, and before you know it, he tells me that there's no way to avoid a strike this summer.

Now I've read about what the players are asking, and in many ways I have to sympathize with them. If they want more in the pension or better severance pay or a higher minimum salary, fine.

But these guys are talking about freedom and I can't buy that. I don't know this guy Garvey who is head of their union, but I do know he's asking too much.

You can't ask them to agree that they won't check your room or that they won't fine you. Freedom's fine, but that's going too far.

That would be like telling Sparky he can't order us to wear ties on the airplane. You've got to have discipline. That's what made the NFL great. You can't ruin that.

A couple of years ago, we went on strike and you'd have thought that we burned the American flag. The public was up in arms. But it was like any other strike.

You don't hear people talking about it any more. It's forgotten, just like other strikes are. Of course, they paid a lot more attention to our strike than they do a cab strike or a strike of electricians.

People have to realize that baseball and football aren't all they're cracked up to be. There are plenty of people walking down the street who earn a lot more than many of the players. We've probably got ten guys on our team who are making less money than most people.

Sure, some guys are paid too much money. Sure, the average salary is high. But the baseball player averages only five years in the big leagues. People don't think of that. And they don't think about having to keep up two homes and having to keep pulling the kids out of school.

Speaking of strikes, I saw three of them today in the seventh inning with two on and one out. That didn't help matters any as we lost to Montreal, 4-2.

June 21
Cincinnati

Ralph Garr is cool. I mean, he is absolutely a beautiful person.

"Man, there's nobody in this game you can compare me with," he's telling me. "I know I hit good. Everybody knows I hit good. It's common knowledge.

"Don't compare me to nobody. I want Ralph to be Ralph. That's all."

And that's just what Ralph Garr is, one of a kind. He and I get along well, always laughing and talking about hitting. We're two different kinds of hitters. He uses a heavy bat, about 38 ounces, and is already running for first base when he hits the ball.

You almost can't walk him. His strike zone is as big as

Frank Howard's was. If he can reach it, he hits it. Then he's off and running, getting more leg hits than anyone I think I've ever seen.

Right now he's leading the league in hitting, up at about .400, and it's getting late in the season to be that high. He's going to win the batting title and he'll probably do it easily.

My first two batting titles, in 1968 and 1969, weren't exactly what you'd call runaways. The championship in 1968 I won on the last day of the season, and the one in 1969 I won on my last at-bat.

In 1969 I was going against Roberto Clemente for the title. We were in Atlanta and I knew the only way I could lose was if I went 0-for-4 and Clemente went 4-for-4.

Well, after eight innings I was 0-for-3 and he was 3-for-3 and still playing his game. Now how did I know this? When I was in the on-deck circle for my final at-bat of the year, a fan who was listening on the radio leaned over the rail and shouted, "Hey, Rose, Clemente is 3-for-3."

That really perked my ears up. Now we already had fourth place all locked up. There wasn't exactly any pressure. We had a man on second and two out and we were winning the game. A rookie was at third and a rookie was pitching.

"What the hell," I said as I walked up to the plate.

I normally wouldn't have done it, but this time I dropped a bunt—a perfect bunt—and knew the title was mine. I had my hit while Clemente finished up making an out and walking in his game.

In 1968 I was less than a point ahead of Matty Alou. He was playing in Chicago and I was going against the Giants and Gaylord Perry.

There didn't seem to be much to worry about. I went 5-for-5 and that should have done it, right? Nope, wrong. Matty went 4-for-4. He actually gained a little on me because he had fewer at-bats.

The next day, the final day of the season, I got a

broken-bat single down the right-field line off Ray Sadecki. That gave me 1-for-3. Alou went 0-for-4 and I had my other batting title.

Of the three championships I won, though, 1973 has to be the one that gave me the biggest kick. The first and the second were more dramatic, but that year I broke the club record for hits with 230.

The old record was 219 and it was set back in 1907. That's something to be proud of.

Of course, I should have broken that record in 1969. I wound up with 218 hits, but I had a 2-for-2 rained out against Tom Seaver, and 1-for-1 rained out against Alan Foster. That would have given me 221.

I got two hits in tonight's game against Atlanta's Carl Morton. Ralph got one, a double.

But we lost, 1-0, leaving twelve men on base.

One of the reasons we lost was because Jack Billingham, our pitcher, couldn't get a bunt down in the third inning.

Darrel Chaney had led off with a single, but Billingham, trying to bunt, struck out. It killed our chance at a big inning, considering that I followed with a single and Morgan walked.

The bunt is one of the biggest weapons in the game of baseball, and one of the things that has hurt us all year. Outside of Gullett, and sometimes Freddie Norman, we don't have anyone who consistently gets the man over on the bunt.

The Dodgers, meanwhile, do and that as much as anything else is the difference between the two teams. To bunt well you have to work at it. I'm certain that next spring it's one of the things Sparky is going to have the pitchers really working on.

Consider how important it is for the Cincinnati Reds' pitchers to be good bunters. I follow them in the order. If they push a runner into scoring position, they have coming up a man who gets from 185 to 230 hits every year. That will lead to runs and runs lead to victories and victories lead to pennants.

No doubt, bunting on AstroTurf is harder than bunting on grass. But AstroTurf is no excuse for not bunting. It just has to be practiced more. If a pitcher can help himself in any way, I can think of no reason why he shouldn't go out of his way to do so.

June 22
Cincinnati

"Gotta do something," says Sparky as he hands me the lineup card for tonight's game. "We ain't going nowhere and we're leaving men all over the bases."

I look at the card. Rose leading off. Geronimo second. Morgan third. Morgan's been moved from the number 2 to the number 3 spot and Geronimo, who had 4-for-4 last night in the shutout to give him a .354 average, is moved from seventh into second.

I go to Morgan. "Now remember one thing," I tell him. "Don't go for home runs just because you're hitting third."

"No chance," answers Little Joe. "I hit 26 last year, but I don't think I can get there this year."

The game starts. I make an out, but Geronimo singles. Now Morgan walks up. Phil Niekro delivers his first pitch, and Morgan hits it into the right-field seats for a home run. He comes back to the dugout and I grab him. "Sure glad you don't listen to me," I say. He grins.

Morgan later hit a sacrifice fly and our other little fellow, Fred Norman, pitched a seven-hit shutout. We won, 3-0.

"Just a hunch," said Sparky about the lineup change.

Keep playing those hunches, Spark.

110

I was the starting mascot on my father's semi-pro team.

The spikes are sharp, and I'm ready.

I figure I was seven or eight, and I don't remember whether I could hit the curve yet.

The Sedansville Civic Club of the Cincinnati Knothole League:
I'm fourth from the left in the back row, and that kid on
the far right, front row, is my neighborhood buddy,
Eddie Brinkman.

This was in my rookie year, 1963, and I'd hit the home run
against the Mets that gave Jim Maloney his twentieth
victory at the Polo Grounds in New York. (UPI)

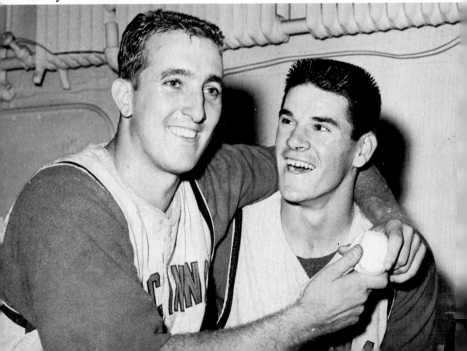

Here's Dad, who made me into a switch-hitter.
(Lexington Herald-Leader)

I was in basic training at Fort Knox, Kentucky, in November 1963 when the word came that I'd been named National League Rookie of the Year. My platoon sergeant, Lester Axsom, needs a haircut. (UPI)

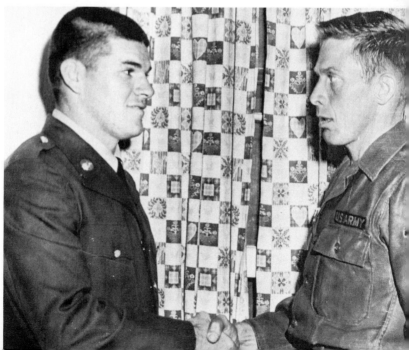

On a windy January day in 1964 at St. William's Church in Cincinnati, Karolyn Ann Engelhardt became Mrs. Pete Rose. (UPI)

Gary Peters and I had something in common at spring training in Florida, 1964: trophies that designated us as the American and National Leagues' Rookies of the Year. (Jack Klumpe, *Cincinnati Post & Times-Star*)

On your mark, get set, go into the 1965 season—I'm flanked (left to right) by Tommy Harper, Vada Pinson, Chico Ruiz, and Frank Robinson. (Jack Klumpe, *Cincinnati Post & Times-Star*)

Karolyn and baby Fawn fraternize with the ballplayer in the spring of 1965. (Jack Klumpe, *Cincinnati Post & Times-Star*)

I'm over the Astros' Ron Brand on the way to a double play at Houston in 1965. (UPI)

This was in spring training, 1966, after Frank Robinson had been sold to Baltimore following ten seasons with the Reds. (Jack Klumpe, *Cincinnati Post & Times-Star*)

The ball was a Tom Seaver pitch that hit me in a game in 1968, the bat hit Mets' catcher Jerry Grote. Nobody got hurt and I got to first base. (UPI)

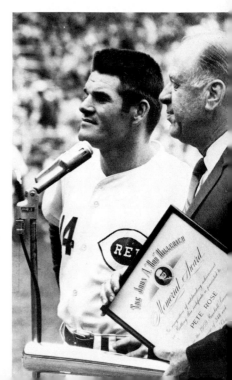

As winner of the National League batting title in 1969 with a .348, I'm getting the formal treatment—a silver bat and a plaque from Fred Fleig, secretary of the N.L. (UPI)

I celebrated the final game at Crosley Field in June 1970
by hitting a triple that wound up with this dive under
San Francisco's Alan Gallagher. (UPI)

My "famous" collision
with Ray Fosse when I
scored the winning run at
the 1970 All-Star game
in Cincinnati. (UPI)

I didn't win this argument—when do you ever?—with umpire Bob Stewart over a ball I claim hit my foot in the 1970 World Series against the Orioles. (UPI)

Like my father taught me, I'm telling little Petie to watch that pitcher from the time he starts warming up until he heads for the shower. (UPI)

The trademark of Charlie Hustle is the head-first slide, and I do it because you don't lose any momentum, and every inch counts. (UPI)

We'd just won the 1972 National League West title in Houston, and while I've got the bubbly, Pedro Borbon (left) and Cesar Geronimo are pouring the suds. (UPI)

This was during the 1972 World Series against Oakland when Gene Tenace made as if to throw to third the way catchers often do to make a pitch look like a third strike. But umpire Bob Engel called it a ball. (UPI)

Even in batting practice, I put everything into it. (UPI)

In mid-season of 1973 I got my 2,000th major league hit in San Francisco, and I'm acknowledging the good fans as Giant first baseman Dave Kingman keeps me close. (UPI)

We're on the same side— Cesar Cedeno, Willie Mays, and I— as the National League gets ready for the All-Star game in Kansas City in 1973. (UPI)

I guess I've got the upper hand here against the Mets'
Bud Harrelson following my attempt at breaking up that double
play in the 1973 playoffs. (UPI)

Ted Kluszewski and Johnny Bench are holding on to me after
the fight with the Mets became a free-for-all. (UPI)

I'm hitting a homer off the Mets' Harry Parker to win this game, but we lost the playoffs. (UPI)

Johnny Bench congratulates me when I was named MVP in 1973. (UPI)

Note the prize-winning form of Charlie Hustle, but I didn't win the prize in the "Superstars" TV competition. (UPI)

On opening day of 1974, an ex-football player named Gerald Ford poses with Johnny Bench and Henry Aaron, but they should have had Jack Billingham in the picture. He served the pitch that gave Aaron his 714th homer, the one that tied Babe Ruth. (Roy Boeh, CSNI)

"You haven't won anything until you've won the big one, the World Series," Sparky Anderson often says. (UPI)

I'm Charlie Hustle. (UPI)

Sometimes, looks are deceiving. Today was one of those days. To the 52,147 fans in the stands, it looked like the Cincinnati Reds were a team of perfection.

We took two games from the Atlanta Braves. The second game took twelve innings and we won, 2-1. Poor Clay Kirby. He's pitched absolutely beautiful baseball for us the past couple of months and is no better than 6-5.

He can't get any runs. Today he worked ten innings. He gave up four hits and only one walk. Of course, he would have won the game 1-0 if it weren't for his own error which let in the run.

He seems to make the one mistake a game he can't afford to make. But damn, he's pitched well enough to be a ten-game winner.

This one was won by Perez with a lead-off homer in the bottom of the twelfth inning against Joe Niekro. It came on a knuckle ball and all I can say is Perez is about the best knuckle-ball hitter I've ever seen. That thing doesn't bother him.

Me? It has always driven me crazy. In 1969 Phil Niekro, Joe's brother, beat the Reds six times. I used to dread seeing him pitch. Not because I was almost certain to take an 0-for-4. But because he'd foul my swing up for a week. I'd change my swing, trying to meet the damn ball.

Finally, I adjusted. I figured the hell with it all. If I was going to go hitless, I might as well go hitless taking my usual swing. So I began taking the full cut up there, trying to hit the ball hard.

I wound up getting a 5-for-5 off Niekro and he hasn't been a whole lot of trouble to me since, although I still believe I'd rather try hitting a hummingbird than a knuckle ball.

111

The first game was interesting because I had a 3-for-3 and because we won, 4-2. It was interesting, too, because it showed that the Reds were anything but perfect.

We wrapped it up in the first inning. Roric Harrison was pitching for Atlanta and I led off with a single.

I'm on first and I see Alex Grammas, our third-base coach, give the bunt sign.

"I gotta get to second," I'm thinking. "Make sure he bunts it on the ground."

First pitch. Swish.

"What the hell's going on?" I say as I take off.

Sure enough, Geronimo missed the bunt sign. He could have hit into a double play. He didn't. Instead, he hit a triple. I scored. He scored moments later. We picked up three runs in the inning and the first game was over.

Roger Nelson pitched it for us, going seven innings and giving up six hits. It took a little courage for that. His arm is still sore.

"I just hope it stays sore all year," he was telling the guys in the clubhouse. "At least when it hurts, I win. It felt fine early this year and I couldn't win a game."

The win evened his record at 4-4. He may be happy, but I'm worried about his arm. He can't throw between starts. He can't work out. And, no matter what he says, a sore arm has to play on a pitcher's head.

June 24
Houston

Sparky is sick. Really sick. You can't believe the way he's moving around. It all started a few days ago with a stiff neck. Then his back got sore. He couldn't move.

Today was the worst. They wanted him to stay in Cincinnati and check into the hospital. He wouldn't do it.

112

"You miss a couple of games and they find out they can do without you," he said. A lot he's got to worry about. He's only won three division championships and two pennants in four years.

For all intents and purposes, Alex Grammas ran the club tonight. The doctors are saying Sparky has muscle spasms, but I have to believe it's something worse.

He looks like a ghost. They have him all doped up.

"How ya feeling?" I asked him tonight as he lay there in the training room.

"Mmmmm, aaaaah," he answered.

I guess that's not so good.

He couldn't even handle his pre-game radio show, cleverly named "The Main Spark." Grammas had to do that.

He's trying. He's in the dugout, wearing a towel around his neck and all kinds of heat on it, but he can't move. Walking's a problem. The neck has his head twisted and his eyes have that Never-Neverland look from the medication.

"Damn Astrodome," he said. "From the heat to the air conditioning. It's no good for me."

Neither was the ball game. Doug Rader hit a three-run homer and Cesar Cedeno hit one with a man on and we got beat, 6-1.

Rader is one of the true flakes in the game of baseball. Funny. He'll do anything, and tonight he vowed to come up with one of his better pranks.

You might remember on opening day this year, Ray Kroc, the new owner of the San Diego Padres, grabbed the microphone and blasted his team right there before the public.

That didn't go over too well—especially with Rader, who was on the other team. "Who's he think he's talking to?" asked Doug, whom they call the Red Rooster, thanks to his red hair and freckles. "A bunch of short-order cooks?"

113

The Padres apparently remembered Rader's remark. They announced today that when Houston is back in San Diego, they will hold a "Short-Order Cooks Night." All the short-order cooks will be allowed in free and will sit behind third base, where they can boo Rader.

Think it disturbs The Rooster? Hell no.

"When we go out there, I'm gonna get me a chef's hat, an apron, and a spatula and go out to third base dressed like that," he said. "They'll love me then."

I believe he'll do it.

June 25
Houston

Alex Grammas is our manager tonight. Sparky went home. Not peaceable, but home he went to Christ Hospital.

He looked so bad last night that Bob Hertzel wrote about it in *The Enquirer.* He must have painted a picture of pain because I'm told that Howsam read it, picked up the phone, and told Sparky he was coming home.

Sparky tried to argue but Howsam wouldn't take a no.

Boy, was our manager ever mad. He spent the afternoon sunning himself by the pool, as he does every day when there's a pool around. The back improved enough so that he was doing exercises.

But he was going home and even exercises weren't going to stop that.

Then the topper came. One of our TV directors came down and he had a Cincinnati *Enquirer* with him. Sparky read the article.

"Why'd he have to write that?" said Sparky, crumbling up the paper and throwing it on the ground.

I don't think he was too happy.

But he flew home and got there in time to watch some of the game on television. He had to like what he saw.

114

Geronimo homered against his former Houston teammates, Jack Billingham pitched a victory over his former Houston teammates, Joe Morgan had a single, two walks, two steals, and scored a run against his former Houston teammates.

That was too much and Cedeno's ninth homer of the year was wasted, the Reds winning 3-2.

Keep up the good work, Alex. Maybe we will find out we can get along without Sparky.

June 26
Houston

Grammas, you're a helluva manager.

"When the hell is Sparky coming back?" said Grammas. "I can't believe there's so much to think about."

Better get used to it, Alex. Sparky's gonna be in the hospital at least a couple of more days.

Larry Shepard, our pitching coach, talked to him on the phone today.

"I'm gonna kill him. I'm gonna kill him," said Sparky, words Shepard couldn't wait to relate to Hertzel.

At least Sparky's feeling better.

The only killing that went on tonight was of the Houston Astros. Concepcion and Driessen homered and we scored six runs in the ninth inning. Final score, the Alex Grammas's 9, Houston 1.

Everything went right in that ninth inning and finally Preston Gomez had to bring Fred Schermann in to mop it up. You could see he didn't like it one bit.

"I ain't no mop-up man," he told one of his teammates.

He proved it, too, giving up a hit and two walks and throwing two wild pitches.

Maybe he should have listened to Ed Sprague, who was our mop-up man last year.

"I'd rather be a mop-up man in the big leagues than a star in the minors," Sprague used to say.

That's a message every pitcher ought to get. Someone has to pitch when the game gets out of hand. They don't allow you to surrender in baseball, although that's what Schermann did when he came in.

June 27
Atlanta

Keep it up, Alex. Another win. Still no Sparky, although the word is he's feeling much better.

Get well slowly, Sparky. We're doing okay without you. Back to six games behind L.A. Someday we're gonna catch them. Hope you're around.

This time we won, 6-3, and Concepcion hit his second homer in two nights. That skinny kid is getting strong.

Just a quickie note here. Danny Frisella pitched two perfect innings of relief for the Braves. I only mention this so I can tell you about Frisella.

He came over to the Braves from the New York Mets last year and got a sore arm. Same thing this spring. In fact, he had a sore everything.

They tell me he spent so much time in the whirlpool that the Atlanta players dubbed it, "The S.S. Frisella."

One day an 80-year-old man was visiting the Braves' camp in West Palm. He had a bad back and Dave Purcell, the trainer, offered to let him use the whirlpool. This old man gets in and while he's in there, Carl Morton, an Atlanta pitcher, walks into the training room.

"Oh, no," he shouts, "Frisella's been in there so long he's turned gray."

Wonder if that's how Sparky turned gray.

116

This was the night of the big Frisbee assault and guess who was in the middle of it.

Me.

It's the fourth inning of the first game of a twi-night doubleheader with the Braves. No one is out and I'm at first base when Cesar Geronimo hits a perfect double-play ball to Davey Johnson at second.

Now on plays like this, I know only one way to play and that is to try and hit the shortstop. That's just what I did here. Trouble was that Craig Robinson, the Atlanta shortstop, was almost in right field by the time I got there.

I slid hard and all of a sudden I was hearing Frank Pulli, the umpire, shouting, "Interference. You're out. The man at first is out."

I jumped up and started to argue, then noticed where I was.

"How can you call that," I said, almost biting my tongue. "The same thing happened the other day and I wasn't called out."

Sure enough, a couple of days earlier an umpire told me I could do the very thing I did. That didn't mean much to Pulli, who had his own interpretation of the rules.

So Atlanta got a double play and that should have made the fans happy. Right? No, wrong. I guess they didn't like the way I went out of the base line.

Now on this very night, the Braves and Lums Restaurants cooperated to pass out 10,000 Frisbees to the fans. It all started, I'm told, when Atlanta publicity director Bob Hope read in a trade magazine that Lums had 10,000 Frisbees and nothing to do with them. What an idea. Give them out at the ball park.

Some idea! Here they come out of the stands. I mean those damn plastic things are everywhere. You can't believe the sight, people screaming and booing and laughing and Frisbees sailing onto the field from every direction.

Donald Davidson, the 48-inch tall traveling secretary of the Braves and one of the best executives in baseball, is up in his private box having a fit while all this is going on.

"Keep those damn things," he shouts. "We can give them away again tomorrow."

The grounds crew did its best to clear the 10,000 Frisbees away, but they didn't get all of them. I know because each of us wound up with about twelve of them for our kids. Kosco needed about 100 of them with as many kids as he has running around the house.

The first game was what I call a good game. We scored five times in the second inning and once in the fifth on Perez's home run, then held on to win, 6-5.

The second game wasn't all that exciting, though. Alex Grammas took his first loss filling in for Sparky, who's still in the hospital, when Buzz Capra shut us out.

Capra pitched as good a game as I've seen this year and I can understand why no one in the league is hitting him. This game went ten innings, finally ending when Dusty Baker hit a one-out homer off Don Gullett.

"Now I know why Sparky's back is aching," said Grammas when it was over. "Maybe I'll just stay as a coach. This managing is tough."

June 29
Atlanta

There was a stranger in the clubhouse tonight. Sparky What's-his-name. Back from the hospital. Feeling great. Not mad at anyone.

118

You can come out of hiding, Hertzel. Sparky says he needed to go into the hospital. Says it was good for him. Wonder how he'd have felt if we'd lost four or five.

He was bouncing around like a spry chicken, which gets me to Mark Hatfield, the clubhouse man here in Atlanta.

The visiting clubhouse man on the road has more than enough to do. He takes care of the uniforms, cleans and shines the shoes, sees that the players have everything they need from cigarettes to Hershey bars.

And some of the clubhouse guys around the league seem to "shine" the shoes with the Hershey bars. At least that's how the shoes look.

The most important thing the clubhouse man does is provide a post-game meal. It could be anything: cold cuts, hot dogs, chicken, even a steak if he's a real hustler and wants to come up with a super-large tip.

Tonight's fare was chicken. At least it was supposed to be. Mark ordered the chicken. It was late coming, not exactly the kind of reception you want in the clubhouse after you've just beaten the Braves, 2-0, in their park behind Jack Billingham. Yes, we can even win with Sparky managing.

Everybody was moaning and groaning until it finally arrived just at bus time. It sort of reminded me of a night in New York during the 1971 season.

The clubhouse man at Shea Stadium is named Mickey and if I tell you that he's something short of the number 1 man in the league, you'll understand.

Anyway, we were playing the Mets and we had a little rain and extra innings. The game was a long one, something Mickey hadn't anticipated.

His post-game meal was going to be pizza and, sure enough, while the game was going the pizza came. Now Mickey had a problem. He had a dozen or so pizza pies, all hot and steaming, and no one to eat them.

How am I going to keep them hot? he wondered.

119

Then the brainstorm hit him. Off he went to the dryer—the same dryer he uses for the jocks and the socks. In went the pizzas, to keep warm.

Fortunately, Jim Merritt was taken out of the game early that night. He came in and saw where the pizza was. He couldn't believe it. Nearly fell over.

Had he not come in early, Mickey would have had those damn things out on the table waiting for us. And we would have eaten them.

Then we would have wondered how we came down with jock itch of the stomach.

Not one piece of pizza was eaten that night. I learned one thing, though. Pizza pies make good ashtrays.

Post-game meals sometimes are interesting. A manager doesn't always like to see his team rush to the table after a loss. I know it really used to bother Bristol. If you got your tail kicked in a game, he didn't want you running to the food table. He took defeat very badly. He couldn't stand for a team to look rotten on the field and then go right into the clubhouse, take a turn, and start eating. He wanted you to meditate a little bit about it.

Sparky's the same way. In 1971 we called a kid by the name of Steve Blateric up from the minor leagues. Now we're out of the race but we're playing contenders and one day he brings in Blateric to pitch against the Giants.

This is the year the pennant was decided between the Giants and Dodgers on the final day, San Francisco finally winning. One of the reasons was Blateric.

He comes in when the game is still close. Then all I remember is Willie McCovey almost hitting one through the wall. Willie Mays hit one on a line over the center-field fence.

In fact everything hit is a sizzler. Blateric gives up about six runs and the heat is on Sparky for bringing the kid in anyway. The game's over and everyone heads for the clubhouse.

120

What does Blateric do? He goes right to the food table. He hasn't even put his glove down. Right there and starts eating, just like he pitched a two-hit shutout.

I thought Sparky was going to go through the ceiling. Next year, 1972, Sparky cut out the food at home.

"You want to eat, go home and do it," he said.

There was some bitching and moaning and it probably cut down on clubhouse man Bernie Stowe's tips. But we won the pennant, which must prove something about a "hungry" player.

June 30
Atlanta

Sparky, don't do it.

That's what I was thinking when I saw the lineup. Perez was on the bench. Concepcion was on the bench. It was as though we were ten games in front instead of chasing the Dodgers.

I really couldn't believe it when he held Perez out of the lineup knowing he likes to play every day. We're off tomorrow; he can rest then.

I just don't think a $100,000 ballplayer should ever rest. Ever.

But Perez was rested. Our chances of winning weren't as good as if he'd played. And what's the difference if we lose to the Braves or the Dodgers? A loss is a loss, just like a Rose is a rose.

We lost. Scored three in the first inning, too, and lost. I opened the game with a single and scored on Danny Driessen's double. That was my last hit. It was also our final three runs off Carl Morton.

Freddie Norman just didn't have it. He gave up two in the fourth and four in the fifth, and instead of carrying all

121

kinds of momentum in against the Dodgers, we'll go in with a loss.

Not that we're playing badly. We've won eight of eleven, which is good. Trouble is the Dodgers have won nine of ten. And we're not hitting. Bench and Perez are in the .260's, I'm in the .280's, and only Morgan is over .300 and he's beginning to go sour.

Oh, well, at least I don't look at this as a crucial series coming up. Just win two, stay seven or so back until we get The Machine going.

July 1
Cincinnati

We were off today. It was a good thing. I didn't have to say goodbye.

Mike McQueen was dropped today. He had fought hard to come back from the automobile accident of a couple of winters ago that nearly killed him. He hadn't regained enough, though, to stay with us through the pennant race. We returned him to the Atlanta Braves.

We also got rid of another pitcher, Roger Nelson. His arm won't come around at all. He can't throw a baseball from home to the mound. He went on the disabled list.

In their place we will have Tom Carroll, a young right-handed pitcher, and Will McEnaney, a young left-handed pitcher. Tomorrow, when we play, I can say hello. I'd always rather say hello than goodbye.

July 3
Cincinnati

Well, we know we can beat the Dodgers. We actually did it today. After seven straight losses we won a game, and I don't

122

mind telling you that I liked very much ending Doug Rau's shutout with my second homer of the year.

It started us off to six runs and a 6-0 victory, which Don Gullett pitched. Of course, we lost the first game of the doubleheader, 4-1, to Tommy John and Mike Marshall.

But now we know we can beat them. And that's important. There is one more game left in this series and nine more with them after that. They are the team we are going to have to beat.

What may be most interesting of all about today, though, was that in the eighth inning I came to bat and grounded to the pitcher. The pitcher was Jim Brewer, the left-handed specialist of the Dodgers. I can't remember my last hit off him.

I'm often asked to name the toughest pitchers I've ever faced and, let me tell you, Jim Brewer is on that list.

I'm a little funny that way. I won't name the same guys that other people will. Tom Seaver is a great pitcher. Fergie Jenkins is a great pitcher. But I always hit those guys. I don't know if it's because I bear down harder or what.

I guess the greatest pitcher I ever faced was Juan Marichal. He had five pitches and he could get any of them over any time he wanted to.

The greatest pitcher I ever faced as far as throwing hard is concerned was Sandy Koufax. No one else came close. And the greatest competitor I ever faced was Bob Gibson.

Brewer, though, is something else. I've just never had any success with him. I never could pick up the rotation on his screwball. I've had success with Marichal's screwball. I've hit Marshall and Tug McGraw.

I mean, believe it or not, I can tell if a pitch is a breaking ball when it leaves the pitcher's hand. But with Brewer I just can't tell. It drives me crazy.

Marichal probably revolutionized pitching. He was

doing ten years ago what everybody does now. He'd throw 2-and-0 curves and 3-and-1 sliders.

Pitching in the National League has become more like that of the American League, if what I've been told is right. It's more a breaking-ball league now.

No one challenges anybody anymore. It used to be that with the count 2-and-0 a guy would throw a fast ball and try to throw it for a strike. Now they nibble with a curve.

Believe me. It makes hitting harder. Nobody has any patterns any more.

I'm a thinking kind of hitter. I study pitchers. I know what they throw and what they don't throw and what they like to turn to in a given situation. When I'm walking up to the plate I'm always thinking about how a guy pitched me in the past.

Bob Gibson, you know, isn't going to start me off with a breaking ball. Other pitchers will.

I like to see how a guy's pitching. Take the Dodgers' Don Sutton. Some nights he's got the best curve in baseball. Other nights he'll throw his fast ball. Or he may have a good screwball. I watch him very closely and see how he's developing. I see what pitch he's getting over; if he's getting one over, why should he change?

I always am looking for a fast ball. I can't hit any other way. I'm not a guess hitter. I've tried it differently in batting practice and it just doesn't work.

Oh, you go up against a Sutton and the curve is on the back of your mind. He'll use it as an out pitch.

I can remember one game I played against Pittsburgh when Dave Giusti was pitching. His out pitch is a palm ball.

He started me off with a fast ball and I fouled it back. Now it was 0-1 and I figured he was going to throw the palm ball. He will 99 out of 100 times.

But he shook Manny Sanguillen off three times. I knew a fast ball was coming. I got one and hit it hard for a single.

That's why Marichal was so tough, though. He could stand out there and shake off signs and you had no idea what he was thinking.

Now I have to start thinking about tomorrow and Andy Messersmith and the Dodgers. We could use a split in the series.

July 4
Cincinnati

You can be sky high in this game one minute and down in hell the next.

Right now, I'm down in hell. We're 9½ games behind the Dodgers and have to start all over again. Happy Holiday!

It wouldn't have been so bad if they had beat our heads in. But that didn't happen. They just did what they do best. For the nineteenth time this season, they came from behind. They got two runs in the ninth to go ahead, 3-2.

In the bottom of the ninth we have two on and one out. I'm up against Mike Marshall. I'm telling myself just what I heard Sparky saying: "He's not unhittable. He's hung screwballs to Perez a couple of times this year."

No, Marshall isn't unhittable, but he sure as hell has been unbeatable. He gets two strikes on me and throws me a fast ball Ty Cobb couldn't have hit. I swing and miss.

Imagine a guy pitching for the thirteenth time in fifteen days and he still has that kind of fast ball.

But his day will come. I don't care what anybody says. He can't go out and pitch every day. I know he keeps saying he can do it and the papers keep saying he can do it.

I don't care who he is or how big he is or how much schooling he's had, he's not going to be able to do it. I just hope when he goes south Brewer's not in the shape they want him to be in.

I'll tell you what kind of respect I have for Brewer. He's the only left-hander I ever went up to hit against left-handed. His screwball just drove me crazy batting right-handed, so I decided to try it. He got me out on a grounder to second. And he got me with that damn screwball anyway.

A couple of years earlier, Jimmy Stewart, also a switch-hitter, tried the same thing against Brewer. He went up left-handed and had better luck, hitting a triple.

Today, though, Marshall is still fresh, and after he strikes me out he fans Ken Griffey and it's over. We're down in hell.

The Dodgers, I guess, remember last year, just as we do. I know Davey Lopes, their second baseman whom Maury Wills called "the most exciting player to come into the National League since Pete Rose," remembers.

"We remember and we're determined not to let it happen again," he told a reporter. Last year, of course, we wiped out an eleven-game lead in the second half, beginning with Hal King's home run off Don Sutton.

The shoe is on the same foot this year but it isn't going to be so easy. We've just got to play better ball. We're not taking extra bases. We're not getting the bunt down. We seem to be sitting back and waiting for it to happen.

We haven't had Morgan, Perez, Bench, and me hot at one time all year, and we need that to go on the kind of streak we need.

And, we no longer have Hal King. Last year's hero again became this year's fall guy. They told him after the game that he was the man chosen to go to Indianapolis to make room for Tom Carroll on the roster.

Some timing. Right after we drop this game. And Chief Bender comes down to talk to him about it, not Howsam. Why does Howsam have to send Bender to do his dirty work?

And why pick King? Probably because he's the one guy

who won't raise a fuss. So King is gone and we're 9½ out and I'm hitting just .282 and life is lousy.

Sparky's going to hold a meeting today. We've just lost three out of four to the Dodgers and he ain't happy. I go to him.

"Why don't you chew me out?" I say. "Give it to me good. You've got to make an example out of somebody and it won't do any good if it's Darrel Chaney or someone like that."

Sparky says no. He doesn't like to get on his guys. He doesn't believe in meetings. He just likes you to go out and play the game and forget it. But this time he has something to say.

He gets up there and tells us we have 83 games left. Then, for a minute or two, he lets us have it. "How can you let those guys come in here and blow us out of our own ball park? I just can't believe a team can come in and blow us out like that."

Then, just like that, he changes tactics.

"Okay, it's over. We gotta forget about the Dodgers. We ain't gonna see those guys for another month. Maybe by that time, they'll have cooled off a little.

"This has happened and we can't change it. If we lose the pennant, I'm gonna take the blame. It's my fault. You don't have to take the blame. I'll stand up and be counted.

"I think right now we have to start all over and set a new goal. We have to win 55 games from here on. If our 55 games, coupled with the ones we've already won, isn't good enough to make it, there's nothing we can do about it.

"Bernie," he says to Bernie Stowe, the clubhouse man, "see that blackboard? Every time we win, I want you to mark

127

it up on the left side. When we lose, on the right. I want us to see how we're getting on toward 55 wins."

Well, Bernie says okay. So we go out and lose the game to the Cardinals. Clubhouse meetings really work.

Managers have different theories about clubhouse meetings. Dave Bristol loved them. Sparky doesn't. Bristol had a lot of them. Every time a team came in to town, he'd hold one just to go over the hitters.

Those meetings were a little ridiculous. They were like every other meeting I ever was in. They'd always say if you keep the ball low and away or up and in, or up and in and low and away, you'd get the guy out.

Hell, nobody would ever touch you if you could pitch like that.

When Sparky loses, he's the same guy he always was. I can't quite say that about the late Fred Hutchinson. He had a temper. It would build up and build up inside of him, then suddenly erupt. When we stopped in Detroit for an exhibition game this year, the clubhouse man was telling me about Hutch as a player.

The runway from the dugout back to the locker room is lined with hanging electric lights, the bulbs just sitting there. Whenever Hutch got knocked out, he'd be so mad he'd go back down the tunnel and swat out every light bulb, just bust them with his glove.

No one could stop him. So the clubby had an idea. Whenever it looked as though Hutch was going to get it, he'd go back through the tunnel and unscrew all the bulbs—take them right out. Hutch had nothing to break as he trudged down the tunnel in total darkness. Not that that stopped him. He'd go in and destroy the clubhouse. Rip his uniform off. Anything.

I remember we were in New York one time and we lost a tough game to the New York Mets in the Polo Grounds. Those were the days when no one lost to the Mets.

The clubhouse was way out in center field, and when the game ended, all the players went there. Not Hutch. He just sat on the bench, steaming.

He turned to Reggie Otero, one of his coaches. "You get out there and tell them bastards they got twenty minutes to get dressed and out of the clubhouse," he roared. "If anyone's in there in twenty minutes, I'm gonna fine 'em as much as I can. I don't want anyone in there. I want them out of there. I don't want 'em to think about baseball."

Let me tell you, in twenty minutes the bus took a hike. There was no one left.

Another time in Crosley Field we lost a game on a ninth-inning home run. Now Hutch doesn't like this one bit. He's sitting in his office, getting madder and madder. Suddenly he just grabs the ball bag, heaves it right through the window and out onto the street. Sure enough, it hit some people leaving the ball park.

July 6
Cincinnati

Today we reached the mid-point in the season. Eighty-one games gone, 81 left to play.

We reached it by putting another mark on the wrong side of the blackboard. Bob Gibson beat us and beat us good, a three-hitter. For the second night in a row we lost to the Cardinals, and it doesn't seem as though we're ever going to get going after L.A. After all, that's five losses in six games. I had a couple of walks and a single, my 94th hit of the year. Not exactly a thrilling start for a guy who's aiming for 200 hits.

But I always have to remember that I'm not accustomed to having good first halves. Last year was the second time that I can really remember doing so. I was .325 at the All-Star break.

The year before I was .288 and wound up at .307.

I'm not worried. I figure I'll get my 200 hits and hit .300 even though my average right now is just .286.

This has been kind of a funny year. I had my best April ever, then the worst May. I can't explain it.

Part of the reason is that we haven't had any hot weather yet. You can count the hot days on the fingers of one hand and when it was hot, I hit. I know we'll have the good weather in the second half of the season, and that's when I'll hit.

Another thing. I've got 56 walks in half a season. The most I've ever walked in my life is 88 times. Maybe it's being MVP. They aren't pitching to me. I don't know. I do know if I didn't get all those damn walks I'd be over 100 hits halfway through the season and with my best months left to go.

Luck takes part in it, too. I've hit the ball well enough to have a lot more hits. In this game, let's face it, you need a little luck. Ralph Garr is having one of those years when he's getting the luck, and he's hitting near .400. Last year I got the luck.

The difference between hitting .310 and .335 isn't skill. It's luck.

If they start falling in, I'm due for a lot of hits. Believe me, they will come, and when they do, it will be in clusters.

One year, back in 1971, I didn't have luck. I did hit .304, but it could have been a lot higher. A writer kept track for me during the season and he had noted 24 balls that were hit hard enough to be hits, only to have someone come out of nowhere and catch them.

Had half those hits somehow fallen in, I would have finished with about .325 or so, and that's not a bad season. Luck.

Right now I'm just looking for one of those good

series—eight or ten hits in four games. If I have a series like that, I'll go right to .300 and then I'll just peck away.

There's no question I'll get stronger in the second half. I always do. I don't know why. It's just my body. I don't lose weight. I keep going when everyone else is wearing down.

Last year was the perfect example. In July and August I hit more than .400. Still, I didn't have a good September.

That's my goal right now, pour it on in September. This year instead of a bad September, I had a bad May. I'll make up for it. Watch.

July 7
Cincinnati

Two things happened today. First and foremost, we turned it around and now it could well be nonstop, all the way to the top.

We beat the Cardinals a doubleheader. Two chalk marks on the win side of the blackboard. And what was it that turned it around for us? Tom Carroll, just up from the minor leagues.

Carroll worked the first seven innings and gave the Cardinals two hits. Will McEnaney, also just up from Indy, finished it off and we won, 2-1. Geronimo hit a homer and double and drove in both runs.

The second game was a whole lot easier. Darrel Chaney, who hits about as many home runs as I do, hit a grand-slam homer off Rich Folkers in the second inning, and we went on to win, 11-2, behind Gullett.

All I can say is that you should have seen Chaney. He reached first base when he hit that ball, watched it go over the fence, and leaped in the air clapping his hands.

That's what happiness is.

"I almost missed first base," he admitted later.

This couldn't be, but it was. A kid from the minor leagues wins the first and Chaney breaks it open in the second with a grand slam. Shades of 1973. Shades of Hal King.

There is hope.

Oh yes, there is one other thing. A total of 46,016 fans turned out for the two games. That shoved our attendance to 1,040,822 for the year, a staggering total.

We're almost 200,000 ahead of last year and in 1973 we drew more than 2 million. This is Cincinnati, don't forget. Not L.A. Not New York. Not Chicago. Little old conservative Midwestern Cincinnati.

I look at it and it seems remarkable, incredible. I thought last year that Cincinnati's drawing 2 million fans was one of the most unbelievable statistics in baseball history. This year will be even better.

July 9
Chicago

There's something about being on the team bus that brings everyone to life. Even here in Chicago, where it's still morning, and you really haven't gotten your eyes open yet.

The rides during the summer are nice because we go past the beach down Lake Shore Drive. You ought to see the broads. I've gone to strip shows where they wore more.

The lake is on the right as you go by and I've always wondered why the bus didn't turn over as the boys slipped over to that side to take in the view. The Grey Line tour doesn't include this.

They notice everything in the bus. Shooting beavers from the bus is always one of the most interesting ways of passing time. You are up high, looking down into the passing cars. And sometimes you see the damnedest things.

Bench is about the best at spotting a beaver because he stands at the front door.

"Step on it, bussie," he'll shout. "I saw white."

"Get your hands on the steering wheel," someone will yell to a dude who has his hand on the girl's knee.

L.A. is probably the best spot for this type of beaver shooting. The bus parks on the street and a lot of guys are on it early, sitting there on the left side. There is a stop light there and the cars pull up alongside and stop.

And you know what kind of dresses they wear in L.A. Did you ever try to drive a car wearing a short dress and keep a guy in a bus from looking at you? If you are a woman, watch the next time you buy gas, too, and see how long that service station attendant cleans your window. If you're sitting wrong, he might just rub all the glass off before he moves.

Now we're stopped at a red light and this gal on a motorcycle pulls up. I don't want to say she's fat, but you can't see the bike she's riding.

They start shouting out the window at her. "Hey, mama, where you gonna be tonight?" Stuff like that. She's a sport though. Smiles, gives the peace sign, and putts off.

Now we're at a bus stop and there's a whole bunch of people standing there, including one young lady who has lovely legs, a nice smile, a good body, and a pretty face.

We start pulling off. I wave to the gal on the corner. I get a wave back.

It's from the one guy standing there. That's the way I'm going.

Things weren't much better at the ball park, either. I go 0-for-5 but we win again, 8-4, for three in a row. The Dodgers have not buried us yet.

I can't believe it. I swung so badly today that I could have gone up there twenty times without getting a hit. But baseball's a wonderful game. There's always tomorrow.

I came down to breakfast this morning and who should be there in the coffee shop of the Executive House Hotel but Ross Grimsley.

I hardly recognized him. His hair was down to his shoulders and he had a mustache.

When he was a Red, he was a winning pitcher, young and a hell-raiser—so much so that this winter we made the deal that was really supposed to help us. We sent Grimsley to Baltimore for Merv Rettenmund.

Sometimes, though, deals don't work out as you'd like them to and this was one of them. Rettenmund hasn't been able to come out of it, hitting .230 and playing very little.

Grimsley, however, has won seven straight, has eleven complete games, and is helping the Orioles in their fight for the Eastern Division title.

And is Grimsley ever happy.

"None of that Mickey Mouse stuff with the Orioles," he says. "They just let you go out and play ball. Have to wear a coat and tie on the road and that's about the only rule. Last night, when the game was going on, we were playing Ping-Pong under the stands."

That, of course, would never go on with the Reds. They pay so much attention to detail that sometimes you forget you earn your money by hitting, throwing, and fielding.

I can remember one night in Atlanta. I'm always having trouble finding my batting helmet. So I go to Bernie Stowe and get a magic marker and on the back of the helmet I write a little "14." Now I won't have any trouble finding the helmet.

I go to bat in the first inning of the game. Apparently they showed a close-up of me from behind the plate, because the phone call comes from Cincinnati.

It's Dick Wagner, the VP, and he's watching the game on television.

"Get that number 14 off that helmet," he tells Bernie.

The Reds are great promoters but sometimes they worry too much about small details.

There are other rules. You'll never see a Cincinnati Red hit a double, then stand at second base and throw his helmet to the coach. You'll never see a guy hitting with his helmet over his baseball hat. And we're not allowed to roll our hats up and put it in our pockets when we hit. When hitting and running the bases we must leave our hats in the dugout.

If you ever go to a game, watch Johnny Bench or whoever is catching for the Reds. If he's the on-deck hitter with two out, he will not go out into the on-deck circle wearing his shin guards. That's not allowed.

I kind of like those rules, though. They're in there, I think, to speed up the game.

Bob Howsam battled against our basketball team. He researched the hell out of that—especially after Bobby Tolan was out for the 1971 season with a ruptured Achilles tendon, which he got playing basketball.

Howsam always has a reason. He researches everything. But that doesn't make him right all the time.

Some of the guys don't like it. Take Morgan. It gets to him. I mean they tell him he has to have authorization to make a commercial, but if they want him to get his picture taken, they tell him to go up there and do it.

It's funny. They do all that worrying about detail and yet we have the worst uniforms in the world. Nobody on the team has a uniform with the top and bottom the same color. The top will be white and the bottom off-white, or the other way around.

They worry about how high our socks are cut and they worry about our helmets, and then we go on the field with white top and off-white bottom. It looks horrible. Poor

Bernie, he goes through hell trying to match up the uniforms.

Anyway, everyone goes up to Grimsley and says hello and shoots the breeze and then it's time to get on the bus.

Rettenmund walks on and Morgan's sitting there in the back.

"Hey, anyway, we can leave Rettenmund here and bring Grimsley," shouts Joe, everybody laughing.

That's cold.

Now Nuxhall pipes up.

"The hell with that. Is there any way we can send Nelson back to Kansas City and get McRae?"

"They wouldn't take him," answers Morgan. "They don't want the doctor bills."

That's the price you pay when you're Roger Nelson and have a bum arm and the man you've been traded for—Hal McRae—is hitting .330.

Oh yes, we did finish off the series with the Cubs happily, scoring a run in the tenth inning to win, 4-3.

July 12
Pittsburgh

This was one of those days when your head is spinning. We had a doubleheader with the Pirates, a makeup of our rained-out game earlier this year.

Before the games start, Sparky Anderson comes up to me.

"In the second game, I'm gonna bat you second in the order, if it's all right with you," he says.

"You're the boss," I say.

I mean I'm considered by a whole lot of people the best lead-off hitter in the National League, if not in baseball. *Baseball Digest* ran a poll this year, asking five top pitchers who they felt was the best hitter in each position in the lineup and I was chosen as the lead-off man.

But about three weeks ago, Sparky dropped Morgan to third in the order. He was hitting Cesar Geronimo and Merv Rettenmund and a bunch of other guys between Morgan and me.

What happened was that they started walking me. I seldom get an intentional walk, but I got five of them since they took Morgan out from behind me. They were even walking me with a right-hander to get to Geronimo, who is left-handed and hitting .300.

"I want to keep Morgan behind you," Sparky explained, and it made sense.

Now Sparky explained to me that he was still going to let me swing the bat. The number 2 man in the order often sacrifices, but with me batting second, that won't happen much. It didn't happen with Morgan second, either. Sparky believes in the big inning.

The only thing wrong with the change is that I know it's going to cost me at-bats. I can't tell you how many times I come up as the lead-off man with two out in the ninth inning and get that extra at-bat, extra try at a hit.

I love to hit, and leading off I know I'm going to get five at-bats on the road. Batting second, I might lose some of them.

He's planning to lead off with Geronimo against right-handers and Rettenmund against left-handers and I'm not sure I like that. Geronimo strikes out too much and never walks. And Rettenmund is a different hitter leading off than he normally is. He led off one game and went 0-for-5 and saw only seven pitches. I mean he hit the first pitch four times. A leadoff man is supposed to make the pitcher work.

The first game becomes interesting because I'm leading off. Sure enough, in the second inning, they give me an intentional walk to get to Rettenmund. He singles and drives in two runs and breaks the game open.

We go on to win behind Don Gullett, 6-0, and I get two hits. The second hit is an infield hit, and for me it's a milestone. Hit number 100 of the season, halfway to my goal of 200.

Jim Rooker is pitching for the Pirates, and in the fifth inning he pops Davey Concepcion with a pitch on the left arm. Two innings later Davey has to leave the game. He goes to the hospital for X-rays but they're okay.

All you can think about is last year when Davey, having just been named to the All-Star team, broke his ankle and was lost for the season. It was just about this time of year.

In the second game, I hit second and get one hit. We win, 4-3. A helluva day all the way around.

July 13
Pittsburgh

The word reached us today. Rooker has popped off and said he hit Concepcion on purpose. Why did he do that? Davey's really hurting.

"You should have heard him last night," ribs Tony Perez, Concepcion's roommate. " 'Oh, Delia. Oh, Delia. It hurt.' He was calling for his wife all night."

The boys were really giving it to Davey.

"I no can play till Wednesday," he keeps saying and Morgan can't take it.

"That's okay. We don't need you. Last year you broke your ankle and we won the pennant. We've just been waiting for it to happen again. Now maybe we can get started."

That's cold. It's also the kind of thing Davey needs. He's the kind of kid who has to be pushed.

"Did you see him when he got hit?" needles Perez. "He is in pain. Remember Dave Bristol? He would say just spit on it. Don't show them it hurts.

"I remember when Lee May got hit in the wrist with a fast ball. He started to grab it and Bristol is yelling from the dugout, 'Don't show them it hurts. Run to first. Don't rub it.'

"Lee, he listens. He jogs down to first. Then, just when he gets there he hollers, 'Oh, hell. It hurts.' And he starts rubbing it and Bristol almost falls over."

Getting hit with a pitch is never a pleasant experience, but sometimes it's funny. About the funniest I ever saw was Alex Johnson when he was with us in 1969.

He got hit in the head twice that year. The first time was with a breaking ball and he just shook his head once and trotted to first base. Stayed in the game. Never even dropped to his knees.

The second time was a fast ball and it caught him right smack in the middle of the helmet, right where the "C" is. Now slowly, ever so slowly, he sinks to his knees.

But he doesn't want to show that he's hurt. So he reaches for the helmet and starts putting it back on his head. Trouble is it won't go on. There's a knot there so big already that the helmet won't fit over it.

The doc comes out and removes him from the game, even though he's arguing to stay in. In the clubhouse he goes.

"Does it hurt?" asks George Ballou, our team doctor.

"Nah," answers A.J. "But it sure was loud."

We managed without Davey in this one. I had two singles and—of all things—an intentional walk. Figure that one out, Sparky. Bench hit a three-run homer and Tom Hall (making his first start of the year) and Pedro Borbon combined to give us an 8-4 win and three in a row over Pittsburgh with a doubleheader tomorrow.

It's Sunday and time for our inspirational meeting. Every Sunday on the road, Larry Shepard lines up a speaker for the day, passing on the word of Christ.

Today's speaker was Walter Stenger, a former tennis player who fifteen years ago learned the word of the Lord. He talked to us about many things, including "Love thy neighbor."

Apparently the message didn't come across too well because in the second game of a doubleheader with the Pirates—the first game having been won by us, 3-2, on Tony Perez's first-inning homer—all hell broke loose in one of the better baseball fights I've seen.

I guess the seeds for the fight were planted back when we first came to Pittsburgh and Dock Ellis hit the first three batters he faced.

Then, Friday night, Jim Rooker caught Davey Concepcion in the left arm with a fast ball. On Saturday, with Davey unable to play, Manny Sanguillen came up to him and told him that Rooker, who is one of those flaky but good left-handers, had thrown at him purposely.

Then came today, Sunday. In the first game Perez hit his homer off Ken Brett. The next time up, Brett knocked Perez down.

Now it is the second game and Bruce Kison is pitching. First he knocks Bench down. Then he knocks Perez down. In the second inning, he comes close to Davey with a pitch.

Davey starts toward the mound, very slowly, and Lee Weyer, the umpire, stops him. The players come out on the field, mill around, then return to their seats.

In the fourth inning, Kison comes to the plate and I think everyone in the ball park knows what's going to happen. Many times I've heard Sparky tell his pitchers, "If

140

you're gonna retaliate, retaliate against the man who threw the ball."

Billingham is pitching and you know he's going to knock Kison down. Sure enough, he throws inside and Kison, having squared around to bunt, takes it in the shoulder.

Now the dugouts are empty again, the players standing around saying nasty things as Ed Sudol, the umpire, tries to control things.

Sparky turns around and accidentally steps on Ed Kirkpatrick's foot. Instinctively, Kirkpatrick pushes Sparky and here we go.

"Hey, leave Sparky alone," shouts Andy Kosco, the mild-mannered, lovable outfielder. He swings at Kirkpatrick. They start going at it hot and heavy. Brett seeks out Concepcion, coming toward him and shouting, "You started this." He gets within range and Dave pops him right in the eye and he winds up with a black eye.

Daryl Patterson, the Pittsburgh relief pitcher, winds up fighting with Borbon. I don't think he'll want to try to do that again. When I look up, Borbon has him on the ground, is pulling his hair and pounding Patterson's face raw.

Oh, yes, Pedro also took a chunk out of him when he bit him on the side.

"He fights like a woman," Patterson said in the papers the next day. "He had my hair stretched from the pitcher's mound to third base. It's coming out in clumps every time I comb it."

Patterson wasn't through with his pain, either. He had to get a tetanus shot because of the bite.

"Like a dog," laughed Pedro.

And what am I doing while this is all going on? I'm trying to keep out of it, do a little peacemaking. I'm walking around out there when suddenly I feel two strong arms wrap around me.

I look up and it's Chuck Brinkman, the Pittsburgh

catcher from, of all places, Western Hills. He's Eddie Brinkman's brother and hell, I played knothole ball with Eddie.

"It's me, dammit," I say, and Chuck looks and lets go.

He had played his entire career in the American League and was in our league for just three days. He looks at me, grins, and says:

"You guys play for keeps in this league."

Then he's off looking for someone else to hit.

Mario Mendoza, the Pittsburgh shortstop, winds up sneaking behind our catcher, Bill Plummer, and sucker punching him. Plummer is no one to mess with, but he never got his hands on Mendoza.

Still, I think he'd better be careful.

"He'd better walk softly," Sparky told me and I don't think Sparky was kidding.

Manny Sanguillen is going wild out there, his goal being to get to Kosco.

"I promised my mother I wouldn't fight any more," Manny later said, "but Kosco thinks he's a big man."

Kosco couldn't believe that one.

"I promised my father I'd never fight anyone I couldn't whip," he said. "So bring Sanguillen on."

Richie Hebner was battling everybody, but perhaps the meanest dude in the fight was Pirate coach Don Leppert. They say Leppert once broke a guy's jaw in a fight with one punch. I believe it.

At one point, he had poor Cesar Geronimo, a kid who spent his early days in a seminary, around the neck and was choking him. Geronimo was going fast, his eyes rolling back into his head. Leppert might have killed him had not someone pulled him off.

And Darrel Chaney. He wound up testing Leppert. The result was that Leppert took more than a little of Chaney's leg skin off with his spikes.

I guess the fight lasted ten minutes. I couldn't see all of it, but my position was no worse than Roger Nelson's. Rog was on the disabled list and had been warned that if a fight broke out, he wasn't allowed on the field.

So, when it happened, he was in the bullpen.

"Hell, I couldn't just stand there and let everyone in the stands see I wasn't fighting," he said.

What did he do? He ran into the bullpen john and had the worst seat of all for the fight.

Fights are part of baseball and often there are some funny stories that come out of them.

My favorite concerns Dave Bristol, back when he was managing me at Macon. Dave loved to fight. Trouble was he never won. Hell, I've seen him have twelve fights and he hasn't won one yet.

Anyway, Dave is coaching third and this fight breaks out. Elmo Plaskett is catching for the other team. A pretty good hitter, I think he won the Southern League batting title that year from Tony Oliva.

He goes after Bristol and he's got his catcher's mask. Well, he belts Dave with the mask and Bristol is down. His eye is bleeding. His nose is bleeding. His mouth is bleeding. There are huge welts where the mask hit.

Elmo's standing over him as Bristol gets to his knees, comes into the classic fighter's stance, looks up, and mumbles through the pain and the blood:

"Had enough, Elmo, or do you want more?"

That's probably how Daryl Patterson felt today.

July 15
St. Louis

The back of the team bus after a winning game is always the liveliest place on earth. This is where the jokers always sit and after a win, they're wound up.

Tonight's was a good win to get wound up about. The fight with the Pirates is a thing of the past and Clay Kirby has just put together a 3-0 shutout.

Davey Concepcion is really going at it, and well he should. He put together two singles and two walks, scored two runs, and now he's chattering as only he can chatter.

"Hey, Yo," he says to Joe Morgan, who didn't exactly have a bad night with a homer, single, and stolen base. "Hey, Yo, I gonna be a superstar."

"Whoever heard of a superstar who hits .260?" ribs Morgan.

"No, Yo. I gonna be a superstar. You wait. When you are 36 and Pete is 39, you will be sitting home watching me be a superstar on television. You see."

"Then what, Davey?" I ask. "Then what do you do when you're through."

"Maybe I be a manager," he smiles. "You can be my coach."

To know how absurd that statement is, you have to know Davey. Just a kid, beginning to grow up, unable to manage himself most of the time, and here he is talking about being a manager.

"Yeah, you be manager and Borbon can be your general manager," I say. "If anyone comes in and gives him trouble about contracts, he can bite them."

"You see. I be superstar," says Davey.

Trouble is, he's probably right.

July 16
St. Louis

"I wonder if he wants it in cash or if I should write him a check?"

Those words belonged to Andy Kosco. He was holding

144

before him a telegram from National League President Chub Feeney announcing that he had been fined for his part in the fight at Pittsburgh.

Trouble was, he didn't know how much the fine was. Good old Western Union had struck again.

"Near as I can make out, I owe him $185,330," grinned Kosco.

Sure enough, where Feeney had written "you are being fined in the amount of . . ." there followed something like 185%&'#330.

"I just can't believe they're fining me," he said. "Do you know how I got thrown out of that game? The fight was over and I hear Lee Weyer, the umpire, say to me, 'You're out of the game.'"

"Why me?" Andy asked him.

"Well, we have to throw someone out and you don't want us to throw Bench out, do you?" explained Weyer in true umpirelike thinking.

"You mean I'm being kicked out because of my batting average?" answered Andy as he headed for the clubhouse.

Sparky Anderson also received his telegram today. His fine was, believe it or not 185%&'#330.

"I ain't paying," said Sparky. "It's up to them to get the right figure to me."

It was the Cardinals who paid instead. We jumped on them for seven runs in the first and three in the second, then coasted to a 12-7 win.

Don Gullett pitched this one, but, as usual, he did more than just pitch. He had two singles and a double and drove in three runs. He might just be the best athlete I've ever seen.

And so quiet and humble. They don't make them like that any more.

That seven-run first inning was interesting because the key hit was a two-run double by Morgan on a 3-and-0 pitch from Bob Forsch, a rookie right-hander. Now I hear a lot

145

about the 3-and-0 pitch in baseball and the thing people want to know is why big leaguers don't hit at the pitch more often.

The reason is that a lot of batters get overanxious on the 3-and-0 pitch and are less selective than they would be on a 3-1 pitch. Another reason is that with the count 3-0, a batter who has the right to swing away often looks not only for a certain pitch, but for a pitch in a certain spot. If the pitch is anywhere but where the batter is looking, he'll take it because he still has two strikes left.

I almost never think about swinging at a 3-0 pitch. I'm a lead-off man and one of my jobs is to make the pitcher work—to throw as many pitches as possible. Another of my jobs is to get on base. If I swing at 3-0 and make an out, I haven't done my job. And that old saying about a walk being as good as a hit is true.

Morgan, on the other hand, is a great 3-0 hitter. He is so selective at the plate that he makes the pitcher throw the pitch he wants or he'll take it.

Letting Morgan hit in this situation was a stroke of genius on Sparky's part. Morgan was facing a rookie pitcher who had none out in the first and men at second and third. He was behind in the count 3-0 and had Bench and Perez coming up. Morgan is a fast-ball hitter and the pitch had to be a fast ball. Morgan doubled and we broke the game open.

July 17
St. Louis

Everyone knows what's going to happen today. Bob Gibson is going to become the second man in big league history to strike out 3,000 batters in a career; a helluva accomplishment.

Only Walter Johnson did it before, finishing with 3,508.

146

Number 3,000 is going to be one of us, a Cincinnati Red. Now no one wants to become THE MAN. But then again, no one really gives a damn.

We get to the ball park and Tony Perez has it all figured. "I got the odds," he shouts.

And so it begins, Tony Perez's morning line on who will become Bob Gibson's 3,000th strike-out victim.

"Geronimo," he says, "you lead off. You are the favorite. Then Rose is 20-to-1. And Morgan is 30-to-1. And Bench, he is 3-to-2, but that's only because he probably will bunt."

Everyone bursts out laughing.

"What if I don't bunt?" asks Bench.

"Then you are 1-to-3," grins Perez and everyone is in stitches.

"Me, I'm even money. I've been helping Gibson for ten years. If he gets to me, there's no reason why I shouldn't help him again. Always I look for that fast ball, right here," he says, holding his hand chest high. "And always he gives me that hard slider. Hard slider."

In case you don't have the picture yet, the Big Red Machine is anything but uptight. We got it together again.

Gibson goes through nine batters, no strike-outs. Three runs. Even Perez hits the ball and Bench doesn't bunt.

Finally it happens. Geronimo, just like Perez said. Strike-out No. 3,000 and everyone stands and applauds and Gibson tips his cap.

Gibby isn't quite Gibby today. He's got the big curve and control and an occasional fast ball. But the hummer isn't what it was back there in 1968 or so.

The game goes twelve innings and we win it, George Foster doubling home two runs to give us a 6-4 victory.

For the trip, it makes nine wins in eleven games. And we've taken ten out of the last twelve. Loose, hell, we're like a puppet on strings.

During the game, Morgan managed somehow to make two errors. Naturally, everyone left him alone in his misery, right? Not on this club.

"Hey, Joe," says Perez, "What were you doing? I look at that one ground ball and you are fighting it. I mean, you are hitting it and it looks like it is hitting you back."

Kluszewski grabs one of those metal ashtrays and throws it across the room. "Clank, clank, clank," it goes.

"There goes Morgan's glove," shouts Klu.

And then the final insult to a man who just made two errors in a game for the first time in four years.

After showering, he comes back and finds a garbage can in his locker, his glove in it.

Home we go. Back to the wives and kids, and what was my wife doing while driving to the airport to pick me up? Listening to the Dodgers play Montreal.

"They lost again," she told me at the gate, "5-4."

So the Big Red Machine, at 2:30 A.M. is walking down the airport corridors cheering. It's 5½ games and don't the Dodgers just feel a little something like pressure now?

July 18
Cincinnati

Who says the National League doesn't have a designated hitter?

We've got one. His name's Phil Gagliano. He doesn't even need a bat. All he does is walk. So far this year, he's been sent to the plate to pinch-hit 28 times and he's walked 13 of them.

That ties the league record held by Jerry Lynch, and it isn't even the All-Star break yet.

Morgan walked up to Gags today, looked him in the

148

eye, and with a straight face said: "Hey, Gags, do you own a glove?"

I thought Gags was going to go through the ceiling. But the truth of the matter is that he doesn't need one. He has played only one inning in the field this year. Just pinch-hits, that's all.

And he jokes, just like everyone else. One night in Montreal, he and Darrel Chaney were having dinner in The Beaver Club. They finished their meal and got the check, $45 worth of it.

"Watch this," Gagliano said to Chaney.

They waltzed off, dropping the check on Larry Shepard's table.

"Ain't we gonna go back and pay the check?" asked Chaney, after they walked out the door.

"No," smiled Gags.

It was Shepard, though, who got the last laugh this time. He signed the check, put Chaney's name on it, and tipped a staggering 25 percent.

"I don't think they'll try that on me again," said Shep.

Neither will I.

Gag's walk almost helped tonight. It came in the seventh inning with the Cubs ahead, 3-2. When Geronimo also walked, we had men at first and second with me up.

Oscar Zamora was brought in to pitch. He's a 29-year-old rookie and if there's one thing I can't stand, it's hitting against a pitcher I haven't seen before.

I had hit against Zamora in Chicago but I got a bunt single on the first pitch. I still didn't know what he threw.

Now I know. He throws a screwball. For strike three. Looking.

It stayed 3-2 until the ninth, when Geronimo again got on base. With the count 1-and-0 Sparky put on the hit-and-run.

149

Geronimo went, but the pitch was almost like a pitch-out, a foot outside. I couldn't hit it, so I let it go and Geronimo was thrown out.

They wound up beating us because I followed with a single, my third hit of the game, and Bench doubled, but we got no runs and lost, 3-2.

Oh, well, you can't win them all. And the Dodgers still are looking back.

July 19
Cincinnati

This was one of those days you have to have if you are going to win a pennant. The load can't always be carried by the big guns and we certainly didn't carry it today.

I was 0-for-4; Morgan 0-for-3; Bench 1-for-4, a single; and Perez 1-for-4, a double. That's 2-for-15.

However, we went to the bench for some help and got just what we needed in the persons of George Foster and Bill Plummer, two guys who don't get to play a lot. Each of them drove in two runs and that was enough to give us a 4-1 win behind Jack Billingham and Pedro Borbon.

Plummer has the misfortune of playing behind Bench and that isn't exactly the most enviable position to be in. You don't get much playing time, but then Plummer is used to that.

His first year in the big leagues was spent with the Chicago Cubs. Leo Durocher was managing then and he couldn't have liked Plum too much. Plummer spent the whole year with the club and went to the plate twice—once in April and once in September.

"Hell, we even played an exhibition game one day and he called a catcher up from Double-A to catch it instead of letting me do it," Plummer remembers.

Leo isn't one of his favorites.

There's an art to riding the pines. It's not easy to stay ready for the exact moment you're needed. The skills have to lessen the more you sit.

I guess the guy who made bench-warming a true art was the late Chico Ruiz, who played in Cincinnati for quite a while. He was a good guy and a pretty good ballplayer, too. He died a couple of years ago in a car accident in San Diego.

Chico was one of those who was happy being a utility player. I guess he was making pretty good money. Maybe you remember his line when Dave Bristol had him in the starting lineup for two straight weeks.

"Bench me or trade me," Chico said. I think he may have meant it.

But when he played, he played hard. He was one of those players who was a Triple-A star and just an average big league player.

I remember Chico's finest moment, if you can call it that. It was 1964 and the Phillies were waltzing to the National League pennant. We're playing them one night and Art Mahaffey is pitching for the Phils.

It's 0-0, one out, and Frank Robinson is hitting. Chico's at third and what does he do? He steals home. With Robinson hitting. A fly ball would have scored him.

It was about the dumbest play I've ever seen, except that it worked and we won, 1-0. The Phils went on to lose about twelve in a row and the Cardinals sneaked in to win the pennant.

Hutch was managing then and he just couldn't believe it. But what could you say to Chico?

What a character. He had himself a pair of alligator spikes and he wore them for The Game of the Week on national television. He had a personalized cushion for sitting on the bench and a little electric fan to keep himself cool on hot summer days.

151

I don't know where he got the stuff, but he always had something to sell: watches, shoes, shirts, anything. If you wanted it, he had it to sell you.

One night we're in Atlanta and he decides he's going to attack Chief Noc-A-Homa, the Braves' mascot, a full-blooded Indian. Sure enough, he lassoed him while the chief was running to his teepee in left field.

The Indian knocked him right on his tail.

Chico was serious about not wanting to play. I remember one night in old Crosley Field, Bristol listed him as his shortstop.

"I no play," said Chico.

Bristol called him into his office. You could hear the screaming. Finally the door flew open, Bristol came steaming out, kicked over a chair, pulled the phone off the wall.

Chico played that day.

July 20
Cincinnati

As team captain of the Reds, it's my job to carry the lineup card out to home plate before the game.

Not that I do it every day. Sparky is a bit superstitious. I'll carry it out one day and if we win, I'll bring it out the next day. If we lose, Larry Shepard may have the card. Or Alex Grammas. Or George Scherger. Or Ted Kluszewski.

And the guy who wins keeps bringing the card out. Logical, eh?

That never could have happened when Dave Bristol was managing the Reds. Now I love Dave, went through the minors with him. We are like brothers.

But he's not like Sparky. Sparky doesn't like to go to home plate with the card. Dave wouldn't let anyone else do it.

When Sparky was named manager, replacing Dave back

152

in 1970, the first thing he did was to select me as captain. Showed right away how smart he was.

Dave never would have named a captain, not if he managed for a hundred years. He had to be the only boss.

That's the reason he was fired—in 1969, with a pitching staff that had arms made out of silly putty. Sore arms were more contagious than venereal disease: Mel Queen, Gerry Arrigo, Jim Maloney, Gary Nolan. At one point, we wound up with just six able-bodied pitchers.

Still we stayed in the race until the final week, dropping out when we lost a doubleheader to the Dodgers on the coast and then being eliminated when a guy named Keith Lampart hit a ninth-inning home run off Wayne Granger to beat us in Houston.

After the season, Bob Howsam fired Dave. He said the reason was that we didn't stay in the race long enough. But Dave Bristol was fired because he wanted to be the boss. He had to run the show in the clubhouse. There was a conflict of personalities and Howsam, being general manager, had to win.

In spring training, Bristol wouldn't allow the scouts and minor league people to run all over his workout. It was *his* workout. Ray Shore, Chief Bender, Rex Bowen—they had to stay out of the way.

He figured Howsam gave him the players, then he used them as he saw fit. There was no communication and in the end, that's what got him fired here. It wasn't that he couldn't manage.

July 21
Cincinnati

Perez had to use the toilet and when he got there today, it was occupied.

153

"Hurry up, Rose," he shouted.

"This ain't Rose," shouted the voice back from inside the stall.

Just then, Larry Shepard, our sarcastic pitching coach, went walking by.

"That's the john, so it has to be Rose in there. He's looking for his stroke," said Shep.

Nice way to end the first part of the season, eh? Well, we got us a win, 8-2, over the Cubs and now it's All-Star time.

Me? I went 0-for-3. My stroke must still be in the john.

July 23
Pittsburgh

Well, everything was normal in the 1974 All-Star game. The National League won—doesn't it always?—and I went hitless.

Twice I went to the plate, and I struck out and grounded out. I own all of one hit in All-Star play and that came off Clyde Wright in the 1970 game in Riverfront Stadium, the same game in which I had my collision with Ray Fosse of Cleveland.

I first played in an All-Star game in 1965, batting three times and showing nothing but two strike-outs and a walk for my effort. The All-Star game, in fact, had been something of a jinx to me. Going into the 1970 game, my fourth, I still was looking for my first All-Star hit.

But we were on my home grounds and I was confident and aroused. After all, the first hit by a Cincinnati Red in Riverfront Stadium did belong to me, a first-inning single in the first game against Atlanta. I was proud of that, just as I was proud of having gotten the last hit in old Crosley Field, the ball park I spent my youth in.

154

The first night in Riverfront, I went 4-for-5 and should have had 5-for-5. I beat out a bunt, but the umpire at first base, I can't remember who that was now, said I was out.

I do regret one thing, though. I didn't get the first hit ever in Riverfront. That really would have been something, owning the final hit at Crosley and the first at Riverfront. That honor went to Felix Millan, then of the Braves, who singled in the top of the first before I ever had a chance to swing at a pitch.

The night before the 1970 All-Star game, I did a little entertaining out at my house. I had two of the American Leaguers out for dinner and some baseball talk.

One of them was the left-handed strike-out ace of the Cleveland Indians, Sudden Sam McDowell. The other was McDowell's rookie catcher Fosse.

That's right. The night before the collision felt 'round the world, Ray Fosse dined with us and sat around my place talking until 1:30 A.M. or so.

Twenty-four hours later, you'd never have known we were friends. That's what happens, though, when you walk between those white lines and start a game of baseball.

I really wanted to do well before the home folks, all 51,838 fans including the then popular President of the United States, Richard M. Nixon.

The Big Red Machine had been the talk of baseball up until that moment, running away with the N.L.'s Western Division, and was heavily represented on the N.L. team, with me, Bench, Perez, and pitcher Jim Merritt. The Big Red Machine stood for awesome power and everyone wanted to see one of the big guns unload.

I was on the bench at the start, not having been voted to the starting team. And what frustration it was for all us Reds.

Through eight innings, Jim Palmer of the Baltimore Orioles, Cleveland's McDowell, and Jim Perry of the Minnesota Twins limited us to three hits. Going into the bottom of the ninth, the Americans led, 4-1, and the Big Red Machine had been nothing but a broken-down jalopy.

I went into the game in the fifth inning in right field. My first time up, I walked. My next time up, I struck out. Then I came to the plate in the bottom of the ninth with the score tied. I struck out.

Striking out wasn't quite as embarrassing as it should have been. I had a lot of company in Bench and Perez. Bench had batted three times in the game and struck out each time. Perez had batted three times and struck out twice.

So it was that as I batted with two out and none on in the home half of the twelfth, the score tied 4-4, the Big Red Machine was 0-for-8 on the night, with seven strike-outs.

Damn, I wanted to do something. It was a feeling similar to the one I had when I hit the World Series home run off Oakland's Catfish Hunter and when I hit the playoff home run off Harry Parker.

What I did was a bit more in character for me. I singled to center. We now had a chance to win, a chance that got much better when Billy Grabarkewitz also singled to center. I wheeled into second.

Jim Hickman of the Chicago Cubs, a late addition to the N.L. squad, was next, and in ten seconds of fury I had become a vicious villain or a hero, take your pick.

Hickman banged a base hit to center. Amos Otis fielded the ball and fired for the plate. I knew it was going to be close as soon as I reached third base and heard Leo Durocher, our third-base coach, hollering "You gotta go, you gotta go."

So, I went. I wanted to slide. I started to go into my head-first slide. The films show that. But, as I did, all I saw was this big mountain. I couldn't get to the plate sliding and probably would have split my head open on Fosse's shin guards.

The only way I could get in there was to hit Fosse full force. I think the throw had me beat.

The collision was something to see, and millions of people did over and over on the instant replay. Fosse crumbled, his glove flying off his hand and the ball rolling free. I was safe, which at the moment was the important thing, and we owned a 5-4 victory.

I took some flak about the incident, about playing such a daring brand of baseball in an exhibition game. Well, I play to win, period.

For three years now I've been criticized about the play. I didn't want to hurt Fosse. I wanted to slide. He's my friend. I was just doing my job; he was doing his.

It's really funny. Opening day the next season we were playing the Los Angeles Dodgers and Duke Sims was catching. The same thing happened. The same exact play. But this time the catcher held the ball and knocked me cuckoo. No one ever said he was trying to hurt me. No big deal was made over that.

Hell, believe it or not, I had a spectacular collision at home plate with catcher Jim Hibbs one time in an exhibition game against our Indianapolis farm team. If you're going to play, play to win.

I was out for three or four days with a leg injury because of the collision with Fosse. He didn't miss any time at all.

But he hasn't been the same since, and the collision probably was the reason. He had a separation in his shoulder and the Indians didn't know about it. He played the whole season with it.

I don't hit in All-Star competition because I must be familiar with a pitcher to hit him. The rawest, rankest rookie can get me out the first time I go against him.

Hell, I own just about every base-hit record for the playoffs but that's because I know the pitchers. It's the way I am.

Take the 1972 World Series. Oakland threw Catfish Hunter in the first game and he beat us. I didn't get any hits but I was sure the next time I saw him I would.

After the game some reporter walked up and asked me what I thought of Catfish. I guess the proper answer would have been to say the man is great, unhittable. Unfortunately, I didn't believe that.

"He's a good pitcher, but he's not super," I answered.

They asked me to compare him to someone and I compared him to Rick Wise, then of the Cardinals, and Jim McAndrew, then of the Mets. I did so because he depends on breaking stuff and control and isn't overpowering.

"There have been only two super pitchers I've ever faced in my career," I added. "Bob Gibson and Sandy Koufax."

I felt that way then and I feel that way now. I had to tell it like it is.

In Oakland, though, Catfish Hunter is a super pitcher and I had belittled him. At least that's what the fans thought. That's what made them mad.

The matter could have ended there, but I didn't let it die. I went out on a limb, something I always do. You see, part of being a winning player is believing in yourself. I believe in myself. If I don't, no one will.

Well, saying Hunter wasn't a super pitcher wasn't enough.

"A super pitcher is someone who strikes out fourteen or fifteen when he blows his fast ball by you, like Hunter said he did to us," I said. "A super pitcher is a guy you don't want to face again. I won't mind it if I face Hunter ten more times."

Then, to top it all off, I sat down at the typewriter and wrote the following in my column in the *Cincinnati Enquirer*:

> And, speaking of doing better, I'm gonna go out on a limb and say I'm gonna hit Catfish Hunter the next time I see him. I really am. I've seen him once and know what he throws.

They've been making a big deal out of what I said about him not being a super pitcher. Well, he's not. He's a good pitcher and he pitched a super game against us when he beat us, but I'm looking forward to facing him again.

And, I know by saying that, it should make him bear down even harder on me.

Poor Catfish. I guess he didn't know what to think. He was quoted as saying, "Pete Rose pops off too much." He said, "Rose doesn't show me any class at all." He added that he couldn't understand how I pop off like I do and not get thrown at by National League pitchers.

Then came the icing on the cake. Here I was out on a limb. The fans were absolutely all over me. And up came game number 5.

I walked to the plate with the boos cascading down upon me. I was leading off the game. Who would win the classic confrontation, Hunter or Rose?

There were still echoes from the National Anthem when Hunter threw his first pitch. I swung and it started sailing toward right-center. Back, back, and over the fence.

First pitch. Hell, I could have looked awfully silly if I'd have gone 0-for-5 but I didn't. I hit the first pitch of the game for a home run.

It wasn't Babe Ruth calling his shot but it was damn near it. What a perfect start on a perfect night. I got another single in the third inning off Hunter and then won the game with a ninth-inning hit off Rollie Fingers, the ace of the Oakland bullpen.

Bench is different from me. That's why he can hit in an All-Star game. He doesn't need to know the pitcher. He just goes up swinging.

Gaylord Perry was working for the American League and I should have known him. When he was in our league, though, he was a spitball pitcher. Now he's really throwing hard. I mean blazing, and I don't wonder how he won fifteen in a row this year.

He used to drive me crazy. He had me totally psyched out and he knew it. I felt he was cheating by throwing the spitter and it would make me so mad that I couldn't do anything right.

I even got kicked out of one game. Gaylord was pitching and he threw seventeen pitches in the first inning. Fifteen of them were spitballs.

I started shouting from the dugout at Andy Olsen, the umpire. He kicked me out, right there in the first inning of a game at Crosley Field.

He picked the wrong night for that, though. This was one of those giveaway nights and they had passed out 10,000 rubber balls, some carrying prizes in them.

Well, I got a run out of the game and all 10,000 of the balls came flying out of the stands and onto the field. One of them would have won a lady a color TV. And she threw it at the umpire.

As soon as I realized that I had to forget about Perry and his spitball, I found I could hit him. I got 5-for-5 to win my first batting title off him.

Anyway, after I'd hit twice in today's All-Star game, I was kneeling in the on-deck circle there in Pittsburgh when Yogi Berra, the N.L. manager, sent Ralph Garr of the Braves up to pinch-hit for the pitcher. I realized Garr would hit once and leave the game. That wasn't right. Here's the man leading the league in hitting and in base hits and he's going to make one appearance in the All-Star game.

"Yogi," I said, "why don't you put Ralph in left field next inning?"

"You don't mind?" said Yogi, who didn't want to hurt my feelings.

"Hell, this is my seventh game and it's his first. Let him play," I said, and that ended my stay in the 1974 All-Star game.

That game wasn't as much fun as some of the others.

You couldn't have fun with the other players during the workout because, to be honest, there were just too many reporters around. And we didn't have any batting practice.

So, the only time you got to know the other guys was in the clubhouse and that turned into some scene. I learned that just about everybody in baseball expects the Dodgers to collapse and expects us to catch them.

They were really on the Dodgers.

"Damn," said Oakland's Reggie Jackson to Steve Garvey, the fine young Dodger first baseman. "I looked up at the board and you guys led by 10½. Then 7½. Then 6½. Now it's 5½. You guys are gonna blow it again and when you do, you'll have to move to the Philippines so they can call you the Manila Folders."

And Perez needled Ron Cey, the Dodger third baseman who last year said when the Dodgers led by eleven games, "If the Reds catch us, I'll retire from baseball."

"You know why you guys lose?" said Perez. "Because you're all half-year ballplayers."

We got to them. I know that. Garvey tried to get to me, but it was no go.

"There aren't enough 3-for-4 days left for you to hit .300, Rose," said Garvey.

"That's the trouble with you guys and the reason why you won't win," I answered. "All you think about is personal goals instead of team goals."

I thought he'd choke, a statement like that coming from me.

July 25
Cincinnati

We may just have won the National League's Western Division today, even though we gained no ground on the

161

Dodgers. It's a feeling you have, the same kind of feeling that was there last year when Hal King homered off Sutton and got us going.

This time it was Perez in the ninth inning of one of the wildest games I've ever been involved in. We were trailing, 13-9, going into the ninth inning. Then we scored five times, the last two runs coming when Perez hit Randy Moffitt's fast ball over the center-field fence, winning 14-13.

He jumped all the way around the bases and the joint went absolutely insane. We had trailed 3-0, 10-7, and 13-9 and came back to win. And the home run came on what was supposed to be a knockdown pitch.

"I look for the slider and then I see the fast ball and I go get it," said Perez, holding court as only he can. "Tremendous top hand. Tremendous top hand give it the power."

After that, the second game had to be ours; and it was, as Fred Norman pitched a shutout. We won two. So did the Dodgers.

But if the Dodgers were watching the scoreboard, they know the Big Red Machine is now in gear and the showdown is going to be something.

July 26
Cincinnati

Had lunch today with Al Michaels, our former radio announcer, and he can't quite believe how bad the Giants have become.

"Can't wait for the football season," he said.

It's a bore when you're with a losing team, whether you're playing, announcing, writing, or just a fan.

I can tell you how boring it is. I was bored stiff today. We lost, 5-4. Gullett got wild in the third and gave them all five runs.

Perez hit his second homer in two days to cut it to a 5-4 game, then Elias Sosa came on and looked like Walter Johnson for four innings, giving one hit.

Oh, well, L.A. lost too. So all we lost was time.

Dick Wagner cut out my tongue today.

In my shoes, that is. Seems I got a new pair of spikes, not bad looking either. Trouble was that the tongues, which flapped over the laces, were white.

Another little rule with the Reds. No white on the shoes. We wear those black shoes that have the white stripes down the side. They must be polished black.

So Wagner called Sparky and today Sparky asked me to cut the flaps off the shoes. He doesn't want the white showing to the fans.

And I'm trying to win baseball games.

Batting practice and Googie, my four-year-old boy, is with me in his Reds' uniform. We're behind the cage, out of harm's way.

"Dick Wagner called and said your boy has to stay in the dugout," says a security guard.

Does anyone wonder why Tommy Helms used to call Wagner "Grumpy"?

Speaking of Grumpy, that's what Morgan was today. He was mad at the official scorer. A night earlier, he thought he should have been given a hit rather than an error. He did hit the ball hard, one hop, right at the shortstop, who kicked it.

Today he's still mad, not speaking to the writer who scored.

Perez went up to the writer before the game today.

"You cost us last night's game," he grinned. "You make

163

Morgan mad. Why you no give him a hit and then take it away from him after the game?"

No one can be too mad today. We beat the Padres, 5-1, and Atlanta belted the Dodgers. That puts us 4½ back and we haven't been that close to first place since May 7. We've won 16 of 21, and in a week we'll be facing L.A. again.

Once again there is a race in the Western Division of the National League. If anyone doesn't believe it, let him look at the standings.

For the second straight day, we won and the Dodgers lost. We are now 3½ games back and we haven't been that close to first place since April 26.

And to think, Mike Marshall took the loss. Still think you can pitch every day, Mike? They've got troubles. Tommy John probably needs elbow surgery and I can't think of a team that can afford to lose a guy who is 13-3.

And Jim Brewer. Remember, I said I hoped he wasn't in shape when the Dodgers need him? Well, they need him and he's in traction. Bad back.

Ah, shucks.

Our game today was what is commonly called a laugher. We won it, 14-1, and wherever it was possible to do wrong, the Padres did it. Morgan was still mad at the scorer. That was good. He hit his fourteenth homer.

Bench had four hits. Geronimo had two more, and another that should have been a hit, a fly that fell safely in center on which pitcher Jack Billingham was forced at second.

Billingham apologized. That won't do a whole lot for

Geronimo's batting average. But then he doesn't need much help, not at .316.

We broke it open in the fifth inning when we scored five runs. Want to know how bad the inning was for the Padres? We had only one hit.

I guess the tip-off to the whole inning came with two out and just one run in. Ken Griffey hit a line drive to Nate Colbert in left. Now no one ever accused Colbert of being Tris Speaker come back to life.

But Tris could have caught this ball today and he's been dead twenty years. Nate caught it, all right. Then, in the most nonchalant of fashions, he reached to take the ball out of his glove. It wasn't there.

Dropping a fly ball is a sin that no outfielder can afford. I can honestly say that the only time it ever happened to me, I had an excuse.

That was 1973 and on national television, the year's first Game of the Week. We were playing the Giants. NBC, in all its infinite wisdom, scheduled a backup game in a place that was likely to have rain in April. It did. The backup game was rained out.

So we were going to play, no matter what. And it rained. A driving rain, the kind that gets in your eyes and all over you.

Suddenly there was a fly ball toward me. I came in and I was fighting the rain and the ball hit in my glove and I dropped it. I couldn't believe it. The first time I ever dropped one and it was on national television.

Okay. I got over it and the game ended and it was time for supper. Karolyn's brother Fred was over for dinner, and he was really on me.

"How can you drop a fly ball?" he said.

He threw a biscuit at me and I caught it. He threw another and I caught it.

165

"How come you can catch biscuits and you can't catch a baseball?" he said.

I'd had enough. I grabbed one of the biscuits and flipped it high in the air. Just when it was ready to come down, I grabbed a glass of water and threw it square in his kisser.

He missed the biscuit.

"That's how I missed the damn ball," I shouted.

July 29
Cincinnati

This should have been one of those fun nights. It wasn't.

The San Diego Padres kept from being swept by beating us, 3-2, while the Dodgers were murdering the Braves, and we're $4\frac{1}{2}$ games back again.

This should have been fun for a couple of reasons. First, I got my fifth bunt single of the year and the first on AstroTurf, a perfect bunt. It's always fun to beat out a bunt.

The single got us going, too. We wound up scoring two runs in the inning, which was one too few off Bill Greif.

Second, I threw a man out at the plate to cut off a San Diego rally in the second inning with just one run.

Let me tell you, one of the biggest kicks in this game for me is throwing a runner out on the bases. I enjoy it more than making an exciting catch and almost as much as hitting.

This time, Dave Roberts was running and Enzo Hernandez hit a single. With a Hernandez hitting, you aren't exactly playing on the warning track and I charged the ball hard and came up throwing.

Perfect and thank you again, AstroTurf. My arm is only average but it is accurate, and on the carpet the ball loses no speed and bounces true.

I've worked on my throwing. I've especially worked on

166

taking balls off the left-field wall and catching guys who thought they had home runs sliding into second base.

A couple of years ago, Dave Kingman of the Giants hit one at Riverfront that he thought was gone. He stood there at the plate for a minute to watch it sail over the wall. Suddenly he realized he'd better run.

It was too late then. I took the ball and made a good throw to Morgan and Kingman was out. It turned out to be a one-run game and we won it.

Tonight's was a one-run game. We lost. I probably won't remember this throw tonight.

July 30
Cincinnati

"Hey, here's my man," I shout at Cesar Cedeno as he approaches while we're taking batting practice.

"Get over here, man. Hey, Soupy, c'mere," I yell to Dave Campbell, one of Houston's backup infielders.

"This man's really something," I say to Campbell. "At the All-Star game, he looks Andy Messersmith right in the eye and tells him that when you guys play them, he's gonna get three hits off old Messersmith and hit a home run.

"So he goes out and gets three hits and hits two home runs. That's my man."

Cedeno grins. "Tell him, Soupy," Cedeno says to Campbell. "I got my first bunt hit last night. My first bunt. My first year in the big leagues, I had 24. But I don't bunt any more. Now I'm an RBI man."

Indeed he is. Eighty-two of them with the home run Cedeno hit against us tonight and that's more than anyone in the league.

Tommy Helms comes prancing over.

167

"What are they doing hitting you second?" asks Helms, who is having some kind of season with a .320 average.

"It doesn't bother me, but it's really hurting my son Petie. We've got the father-son game coming up when we come back and his heart is broken. My wife can't get to him that he has to hit second behind Little Chief (Cesar Geronimo's son). He wants to hit first."

At about this time, Jim Ferguson, the P.R. man, comes walking by.

"What do you have there?" I say as I see him carrying a picture of Davey Concepcion.

"Warren Giles wants it," answers Fergey.

Helms, who always was ribbing Concepcion when he was over here, looks at the picture. "Oh, no, House of Horrors," he grins. "Hey, you should have heard Rich Morales the other night when we're playing San Diego. He hits a line drive past third base and they give the third baseman an error. He goes by me when we're changing positions and says, 'I'm hitting .202, I don't need that hit anyway.'

"Then he hits a line drive, really stings it, right at the second baseman. What's he say to me? 'I ain't gonna win the batting title this way.' "

"I'll say something," interjects Campbell. "I know there's a place for me in the big leagues as long as he's around. They got rid of me at San Diego last year and brought him up. He hit .165."

Denis Menke joins our little group there at the batting cage. Menke quit as a player three weeks ago, giving up half a year's salary.

"I was tired of backing up to the pay window," he explained. "I wasn't doing the job and this game's too good for me to embarrass it. So, I quit."

Menke now is in the broadcast booth with the Astros. That is a classy addition.

168

There was very little classy about the game. The Astros got homers from Cedeno and Cliff Johnson. Lee May had a couple of doubles and drove in three runs, and Don Wilson pitched a helluva game, striking out nine. We lost, 8-4, and this ain't no way to catch the Dodgers.

August 4
San Diego

What we needed today was a sweep of the Padres, a team we should be able to beat whenever we have a must game against them. We won the first game, 7-2. I got sharp for Los Angeles, which is next, with a double and a triple. Dick Baney pitched 4⅔ innings of scoreless relief.

The second game was a joke. Dave Freisleben, believe it or not, shut us out for thirteen innings and we lost in the fourteenth, 1-0. I had two more hits but they proved to be of no value whatsoever.

Now I don't want to say it cost us the game, but in the seventh inning Johnny Bench got himself kicked out of the game. Leading off in the seventh he tried to check his swing at a third strike, couldn't do it and was called out. As he left he muttered some obscenity over his shoulder.

Dick Stello was umpiring and, I guess, thought Bench had said something personal. Anyway, he tossed him.

To be honest, in the seventh inning of a 0-0 game a guy like Bench, or anyone else, should do nothing to get thrown out. The umpire isn't going to change his call, and in a pennant race we need Johnny Bench.

Umpires aren't always right. But, believe it or not, I like most umpires. They've got a tough job to do and, worse yet, a tough life to live.

169

I feel for umpires but I don't feel sorry for them. I think most umpires enjoy the players and would like to associate with them.

I remember the year after Martin Luther King was shot they held a Martin Luther King Benefit Game in Los Angeles and I was invited to play. My wife Karolyn got real friendly with Al Barlick, who was a good umpire.

He wanted to go out to eat dinner with us in Cincinnati but he couldn't do it. I couldn't go out after a Friday night game with an umpire and then on Saturday, with a 3-2 count on me and bases loaded, have him call a pitch that's an inch outside "ball four" to walk in a run.

Society won't let umpires and players get together. Things like gambling make it impossible.

It was funny. When Barlick would come to town, my wife would take me to the ball park Sunday morning, then go over and have breakfast with Al. And I couldn't see him.

It has to be a lonely life.

Umpires make mistakes, just like players do. They know it when they make one, too, but they can't try to even it up. They have to let it slip by.

What an umpire has to do—Shag Crawford does it and Doug Harvey and Barlick did—is learn to bear down no matter what the score is or what the inning is.

If it's 14-1 and I'm 4-for-5 I want him to bear down just as though it were a 1-0 game. I don't want an outside pitch called "strike three" just because it doesn't look like it will have a bearing. I've seen teams score ten runs in an inning. That's the one thing good about baseball. It's never over.

Some of the younger umpires are bearing down now and that's good.

Sometimes the umpires can really be funny. Last year I was watching the Game of the Week from Shea Stadium. They had the umpires wired for sound.

They were out at home plate going over the ground rules and Nick Colosi was umpiring.

"It's a two-way rule on a fly ball," he said to Yogi. "You know the new rule, don't you?"

Yogi looked mystified. "Naw," he said.

"Well, if you hit a fly ball and it hits a male bird, you're out. But if it hits a female bird, it's all you can get."

He really said that on national television.

Funny thing is, I had that happen. I was playing right field in Crosley Field and Dick Allen hit this tremendously high fly ball.

I'll be damned if it didn't hit a pigeon. I caught the ball in front of the bullpen for an out, and the bird, absolutely dead, fell into the stands.

I don't know if anyone ever checked to see if it was a male or a female, though.

August 5
Los Angeles

I finally got cheered in Los Angeles tonight. Not that it was a spontaneous show of affection. But it was nice.

After half an inning the Dodgers put a message up on their message board: "The Dodgers recognize Pete Rose for what he is—a great competitor, a great player, and a great guy. Let's give him a big hand."

And, believe it or not, they actually did give me a hand. They tell me it's the first time anything like that has ever been done in Dodger Stadium and I must admit I appreciate it. I was a little leery coming back here after the goings-on last time.

We came in 6½ games out and felt we needed to win two of these three games. A couple of minutes after the message went up on the board, we were trailing, 2-0, Jimmy Wynn having hit a home run.

A two-run homer by George Foster got us even in the seventh only to have Steve Yeager, a kid from 40 miles outside Cincinnati in Dayton, Ohio, do in Don Gullett with a grand-slam home run. So we lost, 6-3 and fell 7½ back. We have reached the moment of truth in the season—at least the first moment of truth. We must win two of three or forget it.

The time has come to see just what the Reds are made of.

August 6
Los Angeles

Larry Shepard, whose job is coaching the pitchers, probably put it best: "It kept us in the race. If we'd have lost we could have written the season off."

He was speaking of the 200th home run of Johnny Bench's career, which came against Mike Marshall with me on base in the tenth inning. The result was that we finally beat the Dodgers, 6-3, and are just 6½ games back.

The home run wasn't the most dramatic of Bench's career. Nothing will ever top the homer he hit off Pittsburgh's Dave Giusti in the bottom of the ninth inning of the fifth and final game of the 1972 playoffs.

That tied the game and gave us a chance to win the pennant in what was the wildest moment in Cincinnati Reds' history, George Foster scoring from third base on Bob Moose's wild pitch.

And to make Bench's homer that night even more amazing, he was playing with a spot on his lung that had to be removed by surgery during the off-season. He knew about it and so did a few of the guys on the team, but it was kept secret from the press and public until after the World Series.

Bench's homer today came after my single, just my second hit in Dodger Stadium this season. It used to be that I hit well here but they've changed the lights and I no longer can see the rotation of the ball.

This time, though, I saw it and I hit it. It was a good pitch, right about my shoe tops. I'm sure if Marshall had it to do over a hundred times he'd throw me the same pitch. He wouldn't to Bench. Johnny was looking for a screwball. What he got was a hanging screwball. That's just asking for trouble and that's just what Marshall got. The last time I saw the baseball it was disappearing into the bleachers, about halfway up.

August 7
Los Angeles

We got back into the pennant race tonight. And, we got back into the fight business. It's getting so I feel like I should be skipping rope, shadowboxing, and doing roadwork instead of taking batting practice.

Not that I didn't expect the Dodgers and us to get into it sooner or later. It's been building for two years now, with the tight races and the comments shooting back and forth.

This one exploded in the ninth inning. Jack Billingham was throwing a masterpiece and leading, 2-0, the score he was to win by. The runs were produced in the third inning when Morgan singled and Bench hit another homer, this one off loser Andy Messersmith.

The ninth inning started with Bill Buckner getting a base hit. Buckner is a bit of a rednecked character. His temper is flat-out explosive. Two nights ago he was called back for a pinch hitter in the eighth inning and he gave everyone a display, slamming his helmet down and throwing his bat away.

173

Jimmy Wynn hit a ground ball to Darrel Chaney at third, who threw to second to force Buckner. Now sliding into second base hard is one thing. It's something else when you try to kick the pivot man in the face, and that's what Buckner tried.

His foot came up and hit Morgan in the chest. It's a good thing the little guy isn't four inches shorter or he'd have caught it right in that face he's so proud of. I was watching it happen and next thing I knew Joe had thrown his glove down and gone after Buckner.

"Oh, hell," I thought. "Don't hurt Joe. He's taking me shopping in New York tomorrow and can get us all kinds of deals." I was flying to try and get there and help him out. I got there just after Dave Concepcion, who was standing there trying to help out, got tackled by Steve Yeager. Yeager was supposed to have pulled a groin, but he didn't run like an injured man coming out of the dugout.

I grabbed the first guy in blue that I saw and held him, pushing him toward the pitcher's mound. All the while I was still wearing my fielder's glove and I was thinking, "I hope this guy weighs at least 190 pounds or I'm going to be accused of picking on a little guy again."

I didn't even know who I had. It turned out to be Rick Auerbach, a reserve infielder. And yes, he weighs 165 pounds. I'm just glad that he said later I wasn't trying to hurt him and that I did the right thing pulling him out of there.

There's not a whole lot more I can remember about what went on. I had Auerbach and the next thing I knew I was at the bottom of a pile of ten guys. None of them was wearing a Cincinnati uniform. The picture of the fight in the paper shows me wrestling with Auerbach and eight other Dodgers heading for us, all intent on rescuing Auerbach from big, bad me.

This was not anything like the fight with the Pirates. No

174

one was out for blood. There was, in fact, only one injury and that, of course, belonged to Clay Carroll.

"I got hit by the bullpen gate," he proudly declared, showing off a bruised shoulder, the result of the gate snapping into him.

Buckner, of course, couldn't let things rest there. "I'd just like to have five minutes alone with Morgan," he said after the game.

"Any time," obliged Joe.

I don't think it will ever come about.

August 8
New York

This was a day that will go down in history. Not baseball history. World history.

Richard Nixon resigned as president of the United States.

I didn't see his resignation speech. I was watching the Mets playing on television. I thought they'd interrupt the game for the speech but they didn't, so I missed it. I'm not overly concerned with politics, but I do think you have to worry a little about how your country is being run.

I was a little surprised that Nixon resigned. At first I didn't think he did anything, and Jerry Ford didn't seem to think so either. That just shows what I know.

August 9
New York

Sidney Haw drives a cab in New York City. Who knows, you might even have been in his cab. I was today.

I get in, we ride a while, and all of sudden he turns around and says, "Say, you're Pete Rose, ain't you?"

"Yeah," I say.

"I thought so. You're some ballplayer. I recognized your face. You got a strong face."

Thanks, Sidney. That might be the nicest thing anybody said to me in this town since last year's playoffs.

I got my usual booing from the New York fans tonight but no incidents. They were having too much fun watching Bob Apodaca, a rookie right-hander, beat us, 4-1.

We win two in a row from L.A. to stay alive and then come here and lose to Bob Apodaca. Someday maybe I'll understand this game.

August 10
New York

This was a fine night to celebrate. I ended another of those slumps that have plagued me all year, with an eighth-inning single scoring two runs and giving us a 5-3 victory over the Mets.

I had been 0-for-11 and had just two hits in twenty tries since I'd been moved back to lead-off. I wanted to go out and have a nice dinner, and when I'm in that mood I go out with Morgan.

He is a connoisseur. He knows what it's all about in a good restaurant. He had reason to celebrate, too. Three hits and two of the seven steals we had were off Tom Seaver and Company. Lovely.

So we go to this nice little place and the owner sends us over a complimentary bottle of wine. Now I don't drink much and I'm out of iced tea. I want a glass of wine so I grab for the bottle.

Morgan gives me this dainty little slap on the wrist.

"Let it breathe, let it breathe," he says.

"What you talking about?" I say.

"The wine," he answers quite properly. "It has to breathe for four minutes. The waiter will come back and pour."

So I let it sit there. And sit there. And sit there. Ten minutes go by and this waiter is just walking around ignoring us. Finally, I've had enough.

"Dammit, Joe," I say. "Is it through breathing?"

Morgan looks around. "I wonder where the waiter is. I want some now, too."

So he reaches over, grabs the wine, and pours it.

I start to grab for some myself.

"Not yet," he says. He picks it up and smells it. He tastes it.

"Jeez, all I want is a little wine, not a ceremony," I say.

August 11
New York

Johnny Bench is hot. Red hot. He hit two doubles and his 24th homer of the year today. He drove in five runs and tied for the league lead in RBI's. He carried us to a 10-4 win. I just hope he keeps carrying us. Nobody seems to be able to get him out and that's how he is.

A lot has been written about the two of us. I guess I feel I should set the record straight. I've got a lot of respect for Johnny Bench as a baseball player. He has worked hard and that's something I like. He had that good rookie season in 1968 and did something that I believe in. He moved to Cincinnati. He made Cincinnati his home, moving his family here from Binger, Oklahoma, which is a little town he says is just a mile past "Resume Speed."

I believe a guy who is making a lot of money should live

177

in the town where he plays. I was really impressed that Bench did that. You could see right away he wanted to help the town and the ball team. He wasn't going to be one of those guys who makes his $100,000 and comes to the last game of the season all packed and ready to go home.

I took Johnny in right away. We were sort of partners, had the same lawyers and financial advisors. In 1970, of course, he was Most Valuable Player in the National League. He became a big hero here and a lot of people thought I was jealous.

Sure, I had been the star in Cincinnati but there's no way I could ever be jealous of him. We're two different type players. If I were a slugger there might be some animosity. But I'm not. He's the slugger and I'm the singles hitter.

He's helped me make a lot of money and I've helped him. Without me he wouldn't be the RBI leader and without him I wouldn't be the runs-scored leader over the years. I'm smart enough to realize that.

When he was young I treated him like a human being. He came into a situation that was a lot like mine. When he came up he had a lot of trouble with the older players because he was taking Johnny Edwards' job and Edwards was close with all the older players. So I helped Bench and I know he appreciated it.

People keep trying to make it a competitive thing between him and me and keep saying that no team can have two superstars, but that just isn't true—not with us, because there just aren't any similarities between us. He's single and I'm married. He likes to sing in clubs; I don't. I like to go to jai alai; he doesn't. We're two different people, each doing his thing. No, we're not in business together anymore. He sort of outgrew that, had his own ideas. It wasn't any kind of falling out or anything like that.

Socially we're not close, but that boils down to the married-single routine. It boils down to our likes and dislikes.

I just wish Johnny Bench the best. May he forever drive in 140 runs and help us to the pennant. I know a lot of guys who can use the money.

We're back home and Bench hasn't cooled off yet. I know because he told me so.

Seems at three o'clock in the morning there was a knock on the door at his condominium.

It was a girl, who had made a $100 bet she could get his autograph.

"I'll bet that's not all she got, either," I told him.

Tonight Bench had a single, a double, and a walk. Trouble was he didn't have enough support, including an 0-for-5 from me.

The Pirates beat us, 7-4, on national television and we're just treading water. The Dodgers also lost. My, my, isn't it fun to be in a pennant race.

We blew a doubleheader tonight. Worse yet, we were outscored 29-3.

The 15-0 loss in the first game we didn't mind too much. We were supposed to lose that game. It was the annual father-son game, one of the fun games of the year.

Little Pete loved it. He had to. He batted leadoff. For a while there it didn't look like he would, when Sparky had me in the number 2 spot. I didn't mind it too much but it crushed him.

179

"I want to hit first. I don't want to hit after little Cesar," he told me, meaning Cesar Geronimo's son.

The happiest day in Googie's life, I guess, was the day I went back to leading off. As usual, leading off, Petie got a hit. With us fumbling the ball in the field he came all the way in to score, "dumping" Phil Galiano at the plate with a helluva slide.

The second game was something else again. The Pirates let us have it good, 14-3. And it was worse than the score indicated. They had 21 hits. Richie Zisk and Richie Hebner each had four and Al Oliver drove in five runs.

Were the Pirates hot? They were steaming. They've won 22 of 31 games and it all started with the fight we had against them in Pittsburgh.

"I just want to thank Sparky Anderson for having big feet," Pirate manager Danny Murtaugh said before the game, while flashing that big Irish grin of his.

He meant, of course, that Anderson had stepped on Ed Kirkpatrick's foot to ignite the fight. That ignited the Pirates and got them back into the Eastern Division race, a race that's so close no one can figure out who will win.

How bad was it tonight? Well, as Oliver was running out a ninth-inning home run Sparky stuck his head out of the dugout and hollered at first-base coach Jose Pagan, "Jose, tell Danny we surrender."

Actually, I kind of expected what happened tonight. This year they decided to change the baseballs from the traditional horsehide to a cowhide ball sewn in Haiti. The Reds thought ahead and stored up a big supply of horsehide balls, sewn in the good old USA.

Before a game I always go to the umpire's bag and pull out a game ball to warm up with. I like to get the feel of the balls we'll be using in the game.

Tonight I grabbed one. It said: "Sewn in Haiti."

We'd run out of the horsehides and I had an idea what

would happen. The Haiti balls are sewn super tight and they just jump off the bat.

You might remember a year ago Willie Stargell hit a ball out of Dodger Stadium. That's like hitting one out of Yellowstone Park. It was a Haiti ball.

I wasn't wrong. I have never seen so many balls hit hard in one game in my life. Even the outs were vicious. And Stargell hit a single to center that, had it hit concrete, would have moved it three feet.

All was not bad tonight. The Dodgers lost again to the Mets and we're still 5½ back. All we lost was time.

August 14
Cincinnati

Every time I think I'm having a bad year—and .274 isn't exactly what I'm paid $160,000 to hit—I grab a statistics sheet and look at what has happened to Merv Rettenmund.

This winter we sent Ross Grimsley to Baltimore for Rettenmund because we felt we need one more right-handed hitter to throw in the lineup against left-handers. What we got instead was a nightmare. Rettenmund got messed up early and never got straightened out. He went 0-for-2 tonight as we saved one game in the Pittsburgh series, beating the Pirates, 3-2, in ten innings.

That one win was a big one. I wouldn't have dreamed it but the Mets beat the Dodgers three straight and we're back to 4½ out. It bothers me to think we could be 2½ out. But, then again, it has to make the Dodgers mad that they're not seven out front.

Anyway, Rettenmund is now 0-for-his-last-24. He hasn't had a hit in over a month. His batting average is .206. During batting practice he walked up as Morgan and I were standing at the cage.

"Look at him," grinned Morgan, talking to me. "Merv even looks like an out."

"Hey, Merv," I said. "Is that bat of yours a World Series souvenir that you're afraid to break? How many straight strikes have you taken?"

"Just five," he answered sheepishly.

He really needed me and Morgan to help his morale. Still, he's never quit.

August 17
Cincinnati

The Dodgers' breakfast won't taste too good today, if they can swallow it at all.

We won, they lost, and it's back to 3½ games.

The Dodgers have lost five in a row and we're playing like we don't plan on losing. Jack Billingham went all the way for us today and became the first fifteen-game winner in the National League. He's come a long way, all right, since giving up home run number 714 to Henry Aaron on opening day.

Only one thing bothers me about today's happenings. The International Order of Oddfellows gave out two awards before the game. One was to Bill Plummer, the other to Pedro Borbon.

The awards were for sportsmanship.

I guess Borbon earned a sportsmanship award because he's only bitten two people this year.

August 18
Cincinnati

Don't look now but the Big Red Machine is 2½ games out of first place. The Dodgers, thank you very much, got crushed by Pittsburgh for the third straight day. It was their sixth loss in a row. At the same time we were beating the Mets again, 6-3. The feeling is there.

To win this one we had to wipe out a 3-0 New York lead. No sweat, not when things are going the way they have been. Jon Matlack, who in my opinion is the best left-hander in the league right now, was pitching with the score 3-3 when I led off the seventh inning. He jammed me, got one in on my fists, but I fought it off and blooped it into right field. For almost anyone else it would have been a single. For me it was a double.

As soon as I hit the ball I realized it would be a hit and that it would bounce high on the AstroTurf. I also knew that Rusty Staub, the Met right fielder, has a bad leg. Before I was out of the box I had made up my mind to try for two bases. I made it easily and that set up the winning rally.

With two out Perez was the hitter. They walked him intentionally. Had I been on first they would have pitched to him. The intentional walk was followed by a home run by Dave Concepcion and we led, 6-3.

Running the bases is an important and overlooked part of baseball. Not just stealing bases. Lou Brock is great. He can steal bases. Morgan is great.

But there are other important things. One is stretching a single into a double as I did today. Whenever I hit a ball I'm thinking of making second until the defense makes the play. The same goes for going from first to third. That is so important.

I don't take a very big lead when I'm on first base but I don't have to. I'm not planning on stealing the base. All I want is to get a jump so I can make third. I want to make third even if the ball is hit to left field. With one or none out it gives Bench a shot at an RBI just by hitting a fly ball.

With this shorter lead, my first impulse is toward second base. Concepcion, on the other hand, takes a tremendous lead off first, even when he's not stealing. But often his first impulse is back toward first so he doesn't get picked off. It could keep him from making third on a single.

I believe in taking chances. An exciting play not only wakes up the people in the stands, it wakes up your teammates. I like to think that stretching that hit into a double today woke us up a little. We have to stay awake the rest of the way. The Dodgers now look as though they can be caught.

August 21
Cincinnati

I know I've been going badly this year, but what happened last night is ridiculous. For the first time in more than two weeks I got two hits in a game. They helped, too, as we beat Philadelphia, 7-1.

A short time after the game ended, I was sitting at my locker watching television. It was 11:00 o'clock and the news was on. Jack Moran handles the sports for this station and he's always been a nice enough guy, even though you only see him on opening day and at the playoffs.

"I guess they'll be holding a celebration in Cincinnati tonight," Moran said. "Pete Rose had two hits today." Now I just haven't been going that badly.

I haven't been going as well as the Dodgers have, though. For the past couple of days I've been at the park at 2:30 in the afternoon. L.A. is in Chicago playing day games so I sit around and listen to reports of what's happening there. And what's happening there is murder.

Take the first game of the series. Davey Lopes, of all people, hit three homers and had five hits as the Dodgers won, 18-8, with 24 hits. And what did Lopes do when Dave LaRoche knocked him down? Lopes challenged him by going out to the mound.

How the hell did he think LaRoche felt? LaRoche pitched only 4⅓ innings and in that time gave up fifteen hits and eleven runs.

I wish LaRoche had pitched against us today. I got only one hit and we lost, 9-3. I guess there will be no celebration tonight.

August 23
Montreal

As I walked toward the cage for batting practice, I caught sight of Willie Davis, the Expos' center fielder.

Willie, of course, spent his entire career with the Dodgers until this winter, when they traded him to Montreal for a guy named Mike Marshall. Since then Willie has shot off his mouth more than once about how the Dodgers are going to fold.

"They've done it every year, why should this be any different? They've got the same people over there. They can't take the pressure. It's an attitude," he said.

So now we were only 3½ games back and it looked like he was right.

"Hey, Willie," I shouted. "They're trying to fold."

"Yeah, yeah. I told you so," he said.

"If only those Cubs would have stayed out of there," I answered.

"Man, it ain't all the Dodgers' folding. You're playing some now, too," he said.

We certainly are, and tonight was no exception. With us trailing 3-0 going into the fifth inning, I got a one-out single and we went on to score six times on the way to a 10-6 win.

And just to make the night complete, the Dodgers cooperated by losing. Mike Marshall took the loss and we were back to 2½ out.

Bench drove in his usual four runs tonight, three of them coming on his 26th home run. Right now he's carrying us and he may have to get even hotter.

Morgan hurt his hand. In the eighth inning, trying to check his swing, he pulled something in his right hand. If he misses much time it's going to hurt us. He's the one guy we can't afford to lose. Like tonight. All he did was single, double, walk twice, and score three runs. I guess it's up to me to pick up some of the load.

August 24
Montreal

Today's training room argument was instigated by Morgan, as usual. "How much do you think Lou Brock weighs?" he asked.

"About 170," I answered.

"No, no, no," shouted Morgan. "He weighs about 190."

"Yesterday you tell me 200," interrupted Perez.

"No, I said 190," argued Morgan.

The argument was on, one of those meaningless locker room arguments. And Morgan was willing to bet anything that Brock weighs between 180 and 190. "Get a book and check it," he said.

So off we went after a record book. Now you'd think with two radio announcers, four reporters, and two television announcers we'd be able to come up with something that listed Lou Brock's weight. After all, he's only been in the league ten years and he's stolen 88 bases, getting closer and closer to Maury Wills' record. But there is no book.

Finally, after much searching, I came up with a *Who's Who in Baseball.*

"Okay," said Morgan, "check it out."

I did. Under Louis Clark Brock, the weight read 170.

"No, no, no," shouted Morgan. "That won't do. Check me out in there. They have me at 150 and I weigh 165."

Sure enough, I checked and it did list Morgan at 150. Who says you can believe what you read?

"We're gonna call him. What time is it in Los Angeles?" asked Morgan. He was told it was 10:00 A.M. "Too early. Wait a while. We'll call him in an hour."

We never called and we still don't know what Lou Brock really weighs. Right now I don't even care. Not when I finally broke out of it with four hits, the last one being a ninth-inning double that started a two-run rally, breaking a 4-4 tie and giving us a 6-4 victory. Take that, L.A. The Big Red Machine is rolling.

Don't, however, get too worried. Morgan's still hurt. I don't know if he'll be ready tomorrow or not. Hurry back, Joe, we need you.

August 25
Montreal

As the team bus pulls up to Jarry Park, a ramshackle little temporary park that serves the Expos as home, it is immediately apparent that the wind is blowing out toward right field. That means trouble.

The wind in Montreal may have more effect on a game than it does in Chicago or San Francisco. Baseballs hit that jet stream and never come down.

Behind the scoreboard in right is a large public swimming pool, often crowded with youngsters who could care less about watching a baseball game. We pulled into the parking lot and Merv Rettenmund took note.

"I saw a sign up there," he smiled in the back of the bus. "Pool closes at 2:15 P.M. Clay Kirby is pitching today."

The kids in the pool and Kirby had nothing to worry

187

about. He pitched seven innings and allowed only three hits, leaving the game with us losing 1-0. Morgan, as I suspected, was on the bench, but somehow he always has a way of making his presence felt.

In the eighth Ken Griffey led off with a single, stole second, and went to third when Barry Foote threw the ball away. Terry Crowley, hitting for Kirby, walked. Morgan ran for him and stole second.

Then I stepped up and hit a two-run single, my third hit of the game, and we went on to win, 3-1. The Dodgers won, too, so we remain 2½ back.

August 26
Philadelphia

The American Indians, who they say lost as often as the Cleveland Indians, had a punishment for their guilty called running the gauntlet. The Indians, club in hand, would line up and the guilty brave would have to run down the line while being clubbed.

The tradition has not been discontinued. It's just been moved to Philadelphia, where every night the ballplayers run the gauntlet from the clubhouse entrance to the team bus, about 50 yards of bad road.

Every night there are hundreds of screaming, ill-mannered kids out there waiting for autographs. Only there's none of this "Please, Mr. Rose" stuff. It's shove the point of a pen into a player's eye, thrust a crumpled piece of paper into his gut, and "Sign this." No one was in much of a mood to sign tonight. The Dodgers were off, giving us a chance to gain. We didn't do it, losing 7-6 on an error by Junior Kennedy.

Worse yet, I was wearing a light blue suit. I don't mind signing autographs normally. I must sign 25,000 a year. But I don't want to go somewhere with a light blue suit on and wind up looking as though I was used as a dart board. That's what would have happened if I had stopped out there tonight. I would have had little pen point marks all over my clothes, and I'm not about to ruin my clothes to sign autographs.

It's an impossible situation, and if the Phillies get in the playoffs they are going to have to park the bus inside the stadium. These kids were grabbing at me as I walked through the crowd and I hadn't even done anything. What if I had hit a home run to beat the Phils in the playoffs? They'd have torn me apart.

It used to be the same in New York and Los Angeles. But the club officials figured out ways to keep the fans away from the players. In New York the bus pulls into the bullpen and we can sign autographs through a wire fence. There's no crowd to go through. In Los Angeles there just aren't any autographs; the bus pulls onto the field at the dugout to pick us up. That arrangement started early this year when I had my troubles with the fans there.

I figured that as an athlete I have a responsibility to the kids. They look up to us somewhat. This attitude is changing, though. With the reaction of the fans this year, the cruelties, they have taken away some of the obligation we have to people. Take me. I try to get along with fans more than anybody, and I've been treated with more cruelty than anyone in the last fifteen years in baseball.

Still, I don't like to smoke because I don't think athletes should be seen smoking. And I don't think athletes should be seen drunk. There again, I could be in a bar sitting talking to a teammate and drinking an iced tea. A guy could be sitting next to me drinking a scotch. He goes home and tells his kid he was drinking with me all day. It's happened and there's nothing I can do about it.

It's funny. I don't know why people have been on me

this season. Some say it's because of the way I play. Some say they just don't like the way I play. Others say it's because I get into fights. Most, however, say it's because I make too much money. Nine out of ten people don't like me because of my salary, and that's something I'll never understand. I'd never dislike a guy because of how much money he made.

Sure, I know I make more money than the President of the United States. But he can't hit a slider.

Dick Ruthven pitched for the Phillies tonight and he's as good a young pitcher as there is around. He's got a tricky curve ball and that's not too good for the hitter who hasn't seen the pitcher much.

When I get in this situation I turn hard to studying the man on the mound. It's something my father taught me when I was young and something I haven't forgotten. I watch that guy from the time he starts warming up until he heads for the shower.

And when he throws the ball I watch it all the way to the plate, right into the catcher's glove. It's a good trick to try if you happen to be a young player. Watch the ball all the way, even if you don't swing at it.

That way, you will always be watching the ball when you swing, and that is still the most important single thing in hitting.

I remember the first pitch I ever saw in the major leagues. Just as I'd always done, I watched it from the moment it left the pitcher's hand until it hit in the catcher's glove. Jocko Conlan was umpiring that day. He called the pitch a ball, then glanced at me staring back toward him.

"Listen, rookie, don't look back here at me. I don't need any help with my calls."

Help? I was too scared to help. I was just doing as I'd always done, watching the ball. I watched it again on the second pitch, a ball; and the third, a ball; and the fourth, a ball. On my first at-bat in the big leagues I walked on four pitches.

Later Jocko told me he couldn't figure out what I was doing that first time at bat. By the time he told me, though, we were friends and could laugh about it.

Today I watched Ruthven well enough to single off him leading off the game, and we went on to win, 3-0, behind Jack Billingham.

August 28
Philadelphia

The guys were really wound up as they headed for the team bus tonight. The road trip was over, five wins and one loss. We were heading home and it had been just one of those fun days.

It started with rain, calling off batting practice, and that gave me a chance to sneak under the stands and hold a little conference with the Phils' shortstop Larry Bowa and outfielder Greg Luzinski. The last time the Phils were in Cincinnati, Bowa was all over me about his having more hits than I did. It was kind of embarrassing, a .242 hitter with more hits than me.

But I told him I'd catch him and I did. I'm out front now by six hits, thanks to two more tonight that ran my hitting streak to fourteen games.

"And," I said to Bowa, "you didn't tell me you have only 30 walks. I've got 88. That's why you had more hits than me."

191

"I'm a swinger, man," he laughed.

Bill Plummer was catching tonight and Bench was at third. When it came time for Don Gullett to warm up before the game, Sparky wound up in the bullpen catching him. That was the thing that got everyone going on the bus as it rolled toward the airport.

"Hey, Sparky," shouted Perez, "that was a real minor league thing to do. No class."

"What are you doing, getting ready for the playoffs?" I asked. "You getting ready to turn the team over to Shepard? Next time you better take a mask out there with you. Come to think of it, with that face you don't need a mask."

All of a sudden the conversation changed course. We had two guys picked off first base during the game, and the man in charge of first base is George Scherger, a lifelong minor league manager who likes his beer almost as much as he likes to win.

"Can't you see Scherger warming up a pitcher tonight? He'd get hit in the knee in the daze he was in," I said.

"Aw, leave George alone," said Morgan. "He has enough trouble keeping those guys from getting picked off first base."

That brought everyone into an uproar until Perez, noting that two nights earlier Morgan had been thrown out stealing, to end the game at a 7-6 loss, said, "Hey, George, what you tell everyone? Get a good jump so you don't get caught at second like Morgan did?"

Morgan had to agree.

At just about this time the musty smell of human gas invaded the atmosphere. That was all Morgan could take.

"You mean to tell me I gotta wear a coat and tie around these guys?" he said. "Around no-class guys like this I oughta be wearing Levis."

He might be right.

For the past couple of weeks I've been getting ready to move into a new house. It's only a block or so away from my place out in Western Hills and I'm buying it from Marge Zimmer, whose husband recently died.

A few of the neighbors were teasing Marge recently about selling her house to me, a baseball player.

"I could have sold it to Joe Morgan," she answered.

While we were losing to Montreal, 11-3, the Dodgers were getting beaten by Pittsburgh, 4-3. We're still 3½ back, but the magic number for being eliminated is 28.

It's hard to believe. There's only a month to go and this season has just started being fun. My winning streak was stretched to fifteen games tonight with a ninth-inning double and that gave me the league lead in doubles with 32. Maybe things aren't so bad after all.

Before the game I was talking to Dave Bristol when our vice-president, Dick Wagner, walked up.

"Hello, Blade," Bristol said to Wagner.

"Why'd you call him 'Blade?'" I asked when Wagner walked away.

"Because he carries that thin little briefcase with him. I'm sure there's a knife in there to stick in your back," smiled Dave. It isn't too easy to forget when you've been fired.

I didn't spend much time hanging around Riverfront Stadium tonight after we beat Montreal, 10-2. Even though my hitting streak stretched to sixteen games with two singles, no reporters wanted to talk to me.

Not with Bench around. Johnny merely hit a grand-slam homer on an 0-and-2 pitch from Don Carrithers and wound up the night with seven runs batted in, equaling his high for any major league game.

So I headed back for the old ranchero and a night by the radio. The Dodgers are going against Pittsburgh and I can pick up Bob Prince on KDKA fairly well. By the time I got there the Pirates were leading and I just couldn't resist.

I picked up the phone and placed a call to Dodger Stadium. I got right into the broadcast booth.

"This is Pete Rose," I said to a guy who answered and said he was Prince's engineer. "Tell Bob that Pete Rose is listening and to keep those Bucs going."

I figured for sure that message would wind up on the air but I never did find out. A damn storm hit the Cincinnati area and all I heard was static for the rest of the night. I even had to wait until morning to find out we had gained a game and were only 2½ back.

September 1
Cincinnati

August turned into September today and that means there is but one month to go in the chase of the Dodgers—a month in which we must make up 2½ games and in which we must play L.A. six times. This is what it's all about. The entire 1974 season has been building to one month when the world turns its eyes on the Reds and Dodgers.

September got off to a lousy start. To begin with, it was raining and that meant no batting practice. Second, the Dodgers won. Third, we lost. Fourth, my sixteen-game hitting streak came to an end. Fifth, Morgan still isn't ready to play and that brings us back to the pre-game wait without any batting practice.

194

When a guy is paid more than $100,000 a year and doesn't play, well, he does take a bit of ribbing and that's just what was going on.

"We win without you," I shouted to Morgan. "Who the hell needs a 155-pound Judy in the lineup anyway?"

A Judy is a Punch-and-Judy hitter, a term placed upon a guy who hits no home runs. Morgan gets teased about being a Judy even though he hit 26 home runs in 1973 and will come near that figure this year.

"You guys don't need me. I'll just come back when I'm needed. You grow up to be a Judy and you get no respect," Little Joe hollered back.

"Ah, go soak your hands," I said.

"That's just where I'm going," answered Morgan as he headed for the trainer's room. But he didn't get there right away.

"Imagine, Morgan told them on the television the other day that he's an established .300 hitter," I yelled to Bench. "He's hit .300 all right. One time in June, one time in July. He's at .299 now and if he gets one more hit he'll be out the rest of the year."

Bench smiled. "I know how we can get him back in the lineup," he said. "All we have to do is have me hit a triple with no one out in the ninth inning. He'll be begging to pinch-run for me and score another run."

"I've got another idea," I said. "If I get on four times today and score four runs he'll be back playing in no time. I'll have tied him then for the league lead in runs scored."

"Ah," he shouted. "I've been out a week and I've still got more runs scored than any of you guys. Rose, you're nothing but a Judy."

"I've been a Judy a long time and I ain't gonna change now. But I'll tell you one thing. I'm a high-paid Judy."

We should have known what kind of night it was going to be the moment the umpires walked out on the field. They looked like clowns. Somehow they arrived in Houston and their equipment didn't. They had to scramble around for outfits and what they came up with was something short of spectacular.

They were wearing their own street pants, blue Astro golf shirts, and bright orange Astro caps. It was an omen of things to come.

The game was the backup game for national television, NBC having selected the Dodgers-Giants game on the West Coast to televise nationally. But we found a way to interrupt their game.

The situation was like this. Houston led, 4-2, in the seventh inning. I was at third and Morgan at second when Bench hit one off Doug Rader's glove at third base, the ball rolling into short left field.

I scored easily and Morgan came roaring around third. Roger Metzger, the shortstop, went into the outfield and picked up the ball, throwing home. I was right there, in the best position of anyone on the field to see the play. Morgan slid and was safe.

I was getting ready to congratulate him when Jerry Dale, the plate umpire, signaled out. I couldn't believe it and neither could Morgan. He was jumping up and down.

And Sparky, he went bananas. He came out shouting and pointing toward our dugout. "Look at the replay. Look at the replay," he said and Dale refused to listen.

Now Sparky had not yet seen the replay but he was so certain that he was screaming and pointing. Ken Fouts, the NBC director who wound up being on the spot because having a monitor in view of the dugout is forbidden, was

196

shouting to his cameraman near the dugout, "Kick that damn monitor over."

"Not me," answered the cameraman as he saw Sparky coming toward him.

Sure enough, everyone gathered around the monitor and it showed, without a shadow of a doubt, that Morgan was safe and the game should have been tied.

Bingo, Sparky flipped. He started shouting at Dale, and Dale came over to warn him that the next time he shouted at the umpire he would be ejected. So then they broke into the national game of the week and showed the replay again, and Sparky was just standing there yelling, "Thank God for NBC. Thank God for NBC."

"You're gone," shouted Dale as he ejected Sparky.

"What'd I say?" Sparky asked.

"I don't know but you're gone," answered Dale.

For the fifth time this season George Lee (Sparky) Anderson was kicked out of a game and he was right. Morgan was safe. Dale just blew the call. I really believe he didn't anticipate a play and was out of position. He wasn't even in a crouch to call the play.

But the major question raised by the situation wasn't so much whether Dale was right or wrong or in position or not. Rather, the question is whether instant replay should be used on close calls to aid the umpires in their decisions.

I think not. It would do nothing but delay the game. True, it is important that the umpires be right, but to stop the action and watch a replay would be wrong. There are maybe ten or twelve close plays a game and I just can't see the replay being consulted in those situations.

The umpire is supposed to be good enough and hustling enough to make the right call. And if he makes the wrong call, it is just part of the game. They say those kind of breaks even up over a season, although it's hard to imagine how a call like Dale's that helps beat a team in a pennant race can be evened out. Without Morgan's run, we wound up losing the game, 4-3.

To make matters worse for Dale, the game was televised back into Cincinnati and the city went nutty. Even the city council got into the act. They passed a resolution putting the city on record that, among the "whereases," "We Wuz Robbed."

About the only thing that made the night bearable was that the Dodgers also lost and Morgan returned with a single, double, and homer. Some Judy.

September 4
Houston

I'll never forget the look in Don Wilson's eyes. It was May 1, 1969, and the hard-throwing Houston right-hander had just thrown a no-hitter against us in old Crosley Field. One day earlier Jim Maloney had no-hit Houston, making it the second time in baseball history that no-hitters had been thrown back to back.

Wilson, though, wasn't exactly thrilled by the whole thing. He was coming toward our dugout, his eyes as big as saucers, shouting and screaming that he wanted us and did anyone want to challenge him.

He was a wild man, just as he was on the mound as he threw fast ball after fast ball past us. Few people could understand what made Wilson mad. I knew.

The time before we belted him around pretty well, something like 14-1. And in that game, with the score 7-1, I had stretched a single into a double. Wilson didn't like that, saying we were rubbing it in. He didn't like it either when Bench was calling for 3-and-1 sliders.

Wilson was so mad that he called our clubhouse and challenged Bench, saying that he'd get even the next time out. He did, with the no-hitter.

Well, we got even with Don Wilson tonight and I had to feel sorry for him. He pitched a no-hitter and managed to lose the game and not get credit for the no-hitter. Losing 2-1 in the eighth, Preston Gomez pinch-hit for Wilson. Not that Preston had any choice.

A couple of seasons back he did the same thing with Clay Kirby. I'm not sure Preston did the right thing, either. It's one thing to try and win, as Preston says he's doing. It's another thing to take money out of a player's hands and a no-hitter has got to mean money. This is especially true with Wilson, who was having a so-so season and who would have had a third no-hitter had he been allowed to complete the game.

The Astros are out of the race and I don't think the Dodgers would have complained if Preston had let Wilson lead off the eighth. Hell, he had pitched eight no-hit innings and it wasn't his fault that Metzger made a bad throw to let in two runs.

Morgan, who is a close friend of Wilson's from the days when they were teammates, wasn't thrilled about it.

"They're constantly reminding us of what we owe the fans," he said. "Well, the fans obviously were disappointed. Baseball is more than just winning one game. What about the man? There are limits to which a manager can go. And what about the fans? How many of them had never seen a no-hitter and lost their chance? I just can't believe it."

But pinch-hit Gomez did—and in the ninth, with Mike Cosgrove relieving, Perez hit a lead-off single, our only hit.

September 6
Cincinnati

Little Petie sat in our dugout, bedecked in his Reds' uniform,

199

as batting practice was going on. As he sat there, Steve Garvey, the Dodger first baseman, walked by.

"Hey, get me a ball," shouted Petie. Garvey, perhaps thinking back to the days when he was the Dodger spring training bat boy—his father was the Dodgers' bus driver—obeyed.

"Here," he said, handing the ball to my son. "Here," grinned Petie, dropping a potato chip in Steve Garvey's hand.

"Fair trade," said Garvey as he started off.

"Wait a minute," shouted Petie. "Don't hit any home runs today."

I just wish Steve had obeyed the last order. It wasn't an hour later, in the first inning with two on and one out, that Garvey jumped on one of Don Gullett's fast balls and hit it over the left-field fence for a three-run homer. Final score: Dodgers 3, Reds 1. The standings: Dodgers first by $3\frac{1}{2}$ games.

"A shame" were the words I heard muttered in the locker room over and over. Concepcion. Perez. Morgan. Bench. Me.

Baseball, the great American guessing game. As Garvey stepped to the plate, Larry Shepard, the pitching coach, went to the mound. He wanted to slow Gullett down. It didn't work. Neither did the thinking Don did.

Bench flashed the sign for the fork ball. "I wanted to get ahead with a strike. I want to throw a fast ball in on the hands," Gullett recalled later.

He shook off the fork ball in favor of the fast ball.

"I was looking for a fast ball," Garvey admitted. And had the fork ball come? "I'd have taken it," he said.

So has it gone when we've played the Dodgers this year. Nothing goes right. We fought back from $10\frac{1}{2}$ games and we can't quite apply the cruncher. Something always happens. This time it was one pitch, one wrong pitch.

The clubhouse was buzzing today. I wasn't there 30 seconds when Clay Carroll came up to me. "Hey, you hear what Mike Marshall said about us last night?"

"No," I answered.

"He said pitching to us is like pitching to a bunch of high school kids," answered Carroll.

"Where'd you get that from?" I asked.

"One of the clubhouse kids," he answered.

"Oh," I said.

"No, really. And Marty Brennamen says he said it too."

I wasn't going to get too excited about that. I figure the man's so damn smart, he's smart enough not to make a statement like that. Besides, we haven't hit much better against him than a high school team. Last night he came in and pitched two more scoreless innings.

Marshall was infuriated when he heard about the "quote" from Andy Messersmith; he denied he ever said it. Walter Alston didn't like it either.

"Whoever said Marshall said that is a liar," said Alston. "Mike Marshall is too intelligent to make a statement like that. It sounds like a plant to me."

Now I don't believe it was a plant. Sparky doesn't go for that kind of thing. He wants a team that is professional, not emotional, in its approach to baseball. No, I think Marshall probably did make the statement, just as I might be talking to Morgan and say, "That guy is throwing nothing."

I might not even mean it, and certainly I don't want it getting out. But one of the clubhouse kids over there probably heard him say it and repeated it to one of the kids who works on our side, and he told someone and before you knew it everyone was up in arms at Mike Marshall.

Anyway, Marshall was on the mound today in the ninth

inning when Morgan unloaded a two-run homer after I had walked, giving us a 7-5 victory over Iron Mike. All we had to do in this one was wipe out a 5-0 Dodger lead and win it with a cripple hitting a home run.

Morgan's leg hurt so badly that two pitches earlier, trying to check his swing, he fell down. The pain shot through his leg and Sparky rushed out there like one of his own children had been hurt.

"You can't swing. I'm getting you out of there," he said.

"I'm okay," answered Morgan. "Give me a few seconds."

A few seconds later Joe was limping around the bases, getting a standing ovation. The spread was back down to $2\frac{1}{2}$ and we had one more game with the Dodgers at home.

September 8
Cincinnati

The great Mike Marshall misquote turned around to haunt us today as the Dodgers won and left town with two wins in three games, a $3\frac{1}{2}$ game lead, and knowing in a week they'd be looking at us again, this time wearing gray in L.A.

Mike Marshall made us look just like a bunch of high school kids as he came in to pitch in the eighth inning with a man on and a 7-4 lead; he merely retired five straight batters. In the ninth he struck out the side, and if he's getting tired, I couldn't see it.

I had led off the eighth with a home run off Charley Hough. He's a knuckle-ball pitcher but he threw me a fast ball. I knew it was coming and unloaded, my third homer of the year. Two of them have come against L.A. With Hough, I can tell when he's throwing a knuckle ball. Trouble is, if the damn thing knuckles it doesn't make a bit of difference.

202

That, though, was to be our last hit. The rest of the day belonged to Marshall, who broke his own record for most appearances with his 93rd.

The number that bothers me, though, isn't 93. It's 19, the Dodgers' magic number for clinching the title.

September 10
Cincinnati

Sometimes it's better to keep your big mouth shut instead of telling the world the truth. We finished a sweep of the Padres today with a 5-2 victory. Don Gullett went all the way, struck out eleven and allowed six hits.

And after it was all over, someone asked me about the Padres. "They're demoralized over there," I said. "It looks like they're defeated before the start of the game. That's too bad, too, because they have some good players over there."

That's how I saw things. They were going through the motions and it didn't look like they cared who knew it. That's why I said it. I didn't think it would get them all upset but it did.

If I thought it was in my power to inspire them, I would have. Hell, they've got seven games left with the Dodgers and if anything's working against us it's that. The best we can hope for is the Padres to win two of those games and, looking as dead as they look, they probably won't do that. They haven't beaten L.A. yet this year.

September 12
Cincinnati

Bring on the Dodgers. That's what was running through my mind as I sat by my locker at the far end of the Reds' locker room, a doubleheader sweep of the Atlanta Braves fresh in my mind.

"We're gonna get 'em," I said to Morgan. "I can feel it. It's there. There's no way they can beat us."

"I know what you mean," he said as he fiddled with this little book of his. He was entering his return to action in the second game, having played four innings and gotten two hits.

Morgan still can barely move but he's going to give it a try against the Dodgers. We need him in there. He still can swing the bat and what everyone forgets is that he's the best second baseman in the league.

In this little book of his he keeps a log of everything that has happened during the season. Each of his at-bats, what he hit, whom he faced, stolen bases, plays in the field. He knows who got him out and how and he knows why. He studies the damn thing, with all its notes, and it doesn't hurt him at all when it comes time for contract talks, either. He has the facts and figures about himself and he can throw them out at the drop of a hat.

I guess every player keeps his own little book in his own way. Mine's in my head. I can tell you what I did against every pitcher I faced for the last month, right down to the pitch and the count. I know what a guy throws and when he's likely to throw a certain pitch.

The first game was something. Darrell Evans hit a grand-slam homer for the Braves in the second to give them a 4-0 lead. I wasn't worried. We always score against Atlanta and especially against Ron Reed, who is a good pitcher but who always seems to get bombed against us.

Hell, he even gave up a home run to Woody Woodward in 1970. Woody was our shortstop then and it was to be the only home run of his career. Reed also gave up the first home run hit by a Red in Riverfront Stadium, and that was hit by someone less than a power hitter, Tommy Helms.

So, it didn't surprise me at all when Cesar Geronimo

came back in the bottom of the second and hit another grand slam to put us ahead, 5-4. I guess it wasn't surprising, either, that Reed was a little mad in the third inning. With two out and none on he hit Concepcion with a pitch and now Davey was less than happy. He had some words with Reed, big Ron shouting, "I didn't mean to do it."

By this time we had a rookie pitcher by the name of Rawlins Jackson Eastwick III on the mound, making his big league debut. He had pitched all of one inning and when Reed came to the plate Davey came to the mound.

"Knock his head off," Davey commanded. Imagine how Eastwick had to feel in his first game being ordered by the shortstop to hit the pitcher. Fortunately for Reed, there was a man on and none out and Eastwick couldn't afford to throw at the pitcher. So Reed survived, but Davey remembers.

He's been thrown at a lot this year. I guess there are a lot of reasons. He takes his time getting ready at the plate and he's a base stealer. And, if you don't know him, you get the impression he's a cocky Venezuelan, which he really isn't.

He seems to rub pitchers the wrong way, and that can be dangerous in the big leagues. They still will throw at you.

Two wins over the Braves and heading West, 3½ games out of first place and fully expecting to win at least two, maybe three, in Dodger Stadium. This is what baseball's all about.

September 14
Los Angeles

The fans loved it. It was the seventh inning and I had just hit a slashing line drive—right at Davey Lopes, the Dodger second baseman. I just got tired of this crap all the time and I slammed the bat to the ground.

That's all they needed. They were really on me. And I sure needed Steve Garvey, shouting from first base, "Stay with 'em." That out, though, made me 2-for-35 in Dodger Stadium and I've hit the ball better than that. I was 0-for-9 in the series and I'd hit the ball hard five times.

I'd always felt that the way to hit in Dodger Stadium was hard and on the ground because of the hard infield. That's the way that's supposed to be successful here, but every time I hit one like that it's right at somebody. Frustration.

So the fans started singing, "Goodbye, Peter, goodbye Peter, goodbye Peter, we hate to see you go."

I loved every minute of it. After all, on their home field at the time when we had to win, that's just what we were doing. This time it was 4-2 and we knew they were shaky, especially when Marshall was called into the game in the fifth inning.

That we hardly believed. After all, he had thrown 25 minutes of batting practice before the game. He's a machine. He throws 25 minutes of batting practice, then comes in and pitches five innings of three-hit ball, giving up only a home run to Morgan.

"That's all for show. He can't really think he's gotta throw batting practice," I said to Bench.

"I don't know. I don't know," he answered.

Could it be that Mike Marshall tries to psyche out the opposition by throwing batting practice before a game? I'm beginning to think so.

Anyway, we moved to within $1\frac{1}{2}$ games of first place. That's as close as we've been since April 12. One more win here and there will be no stopping the Big Red Machine.

September 15
Los Angeles

The season turned around today in the most crucial game of

the year. This was the day we blew it. We let the Dodgers get away just when we had them on the ropes, ready to go under.

Our two wins in two days had gotten the message across. We were 1½ games back and with a victory would have cut it to ½ game. The Dodgers were standing around waiting to get beaten. They seemed to know it was inevitable.

Don Sutton, who had emerged as the Dodger ace, was pitching against Freddie Norman and, believe me, the Dodgers were just waiting to go under. If we could have beaten Sutton, the guy they were looking to as the one savior they had left, they would have crumbled like a stale cookie.

Our chances came in the fifth and sixth innings. In the fifth Norman singled to score Cesar Geronimo with two out, giving us a 1-0 lead. You looked over into their dugout and all you saw was one gigantic frown, stretching from one end of the dugout to the other.

"We've got 'em," I said to Morgan. I really believed it. Then I went up and walked and so did Morgan, loading the bases for Bench.

I don't want to get on Bench here. He's had a helluva season, led the league in runs batted in, played almost every day, and been our big man in the clutch. The count on Bench went to 3-and-1, and had Sutton walked him he would have been gone. Alston was ready to come and get Sutton, and if we knocked Sutton out, the entire pennant race would have turned around.

Sutton had to throw a fast ball to Bench and Johnny knew it. The pitch came in, and for one delirious moment at second base my heart leaped because I saw it was high and inside, a ball. But all of a sudden Bench swung and fouled it off.

You can't blame John for swinging at the ball. As aggressive as he is, he's got to be looking for a pitch to hit.

He's paid a lot of money to hit at 3-and-1 fast balls. But this was ball four and it turned out to be a foul ball.

Now it was full count and Sutton wound up and threw an impossible pitch. "The only damn curve he threw all game," was the way Bench later described it.

The pitch caught Bench completely by surprise and he took it for strike three. Once again, you can't blame him for not hitting the pitch. So we only scored one run that inning, but it was in the next inning that we lost the pennant we were supposed to win.

It was the sixth, one out and the bases loaded on a double by Driessen, a single by Geronimo, and a walk to Concepcion. Ken Griffey was the hitter, a pretty tight spot for a kid who spent part of the year at Indianapolis and who is hitting not much over .200. But we didn't need a hit here. Just a fly ball or a ground ball. As fast as Griffey is—and he's one of the three fastest men in baseball—he'll never be doubled.

If we had scored there it would have been 2-0 and given Freddie some kind of lift, not that he needed one with a one-hitter working. A ground ball, a fly ball, and they would have died. Believe me.

But Sutton didn't let Griffey drive in the run. He popped him to short and that was the pennant, ending just the way it has all year. A man on third, less than two out, and we don't get him in. Execution is what beat us, and it's something we'd better work on next season.

The following inning the Dodgers took the lead, the two men who scored not even hitting the ball. Bill Buckner got nicked by a pitch and Jimmy Wynn walked, both of them scoring as Garvey doubled. That made me mad. I couldn't even say, "Stay with 'em."

In the seventh Wynn unloaded a grand-slam homer and that just crushed us. It was over, not because we had quit but

208

because the Dodgers hadn't. Winning that game was the lift they needed. It kept them from quitting.

We had taken two out of three and gained a game, cutting it to 2½, and really no one was too depressed, although everyone realized we didn't hammer the nail into the coffin.

"We had 'em. We had 'em. One hit and they quit. They flat out quit," muttered Sparky as the bus rolled to San Diego. Ah, yes, San Diego. Three lovely games coming up with the lowly Padres while the Dodgers played Houston. We still had life. At least we thought so.

Then we pulled into Town and Country, our motel. "Oh, hell, even the hotel thinks we're dead," I said as I looked at the signboard out front.

"Welcome, Casket Manufacturers," it said.

Wonder if the Dodgers paid to have that sign put up.

September 17
San Diego

All of a sudden Pete Rose has inspired the San Diego Padres to heights they've never before reached. Who said so? John McNamara, the Padres' manager, that's who.

Last night, when we beat the Padres, they weren't so inspired. Tonight they knocked us off 5-1 with Bill Greif pitching a helluva game. And what turns up on the Padres' locker room wall? That clipping from a week ago when I said the Padres looked like they were beaten before they went out on the field.

"Our team never has quit hustling," said McNamara, who has watched them hustle all the way to 100 losses. Oh, well, now they'll blame Pete Rose for costing the Reds the pennant.

If any one play is going to stand out in my mind from this season, if any one play is going to be the one that winds up costing us the championship, it is the play that happened tonight.

With the Reds losing, 3-2, in the sixth inning, Roger Freed, who had just been called up from Indianapolis, unloaded a three-run pinch-hit homer and it looked as though we were going to win while the Dodgers were losing to Houston.

Our lead stayed 5-3 until the seventh inning. Fred Kendall drew a lead-off walk and was run for by Dave Roberts. Clarence Gaston pinch-hit and Sparky brought Clay Carroll in to pitch.

Willie McCovey and Bobby Tolan both were on the bench and both are left-handed, but for some reason only McNamara knows, he let Gaston hit. And Carroll threw a perfect pitch, breaking Gaston's bat and getting a perfect double-play ball to Darrel Chaney at third base.

Chaney, who had started the game at second base but moved to third when Junior Kennedy came in—a move I questioned, but then I'm not about to second-guess Sparky now—made a perfect throw to Kennedy. That's when the world came to an end.

Kennedy, a rookie, missed the ball. The Padres wound up with men at second and third, went on to score three runs, and won the game, 6-5. It killed us, absolutely killed the Reds.

Errors are part of the game and you know they are going to be made. But this was one error that can't be made in a situation like that, not if a team is going to win the Western Division championship of the National League.

Kennedy was heartbroken and I had to feel sorry for the

210

kid. He didn't sleep at all, just sat there in his room and moped and thought about things like the end of the world.

Things haven't been bad enough for us, losing two out of three to the Padres. Now they go to rock bottom. Oh, we won the game, beating the Giants, 8-2. That wasn't the problem.

The problem was that Sparky picked today to let us know he was unhappy and, to be honest, I can't blame him. We were ahead, 6-0, in the third when first Danny Driessen and then Davey Concepcion made errors.

Sparky looked out there and Davey was giggling, and that was more than the man could take. He flipped. He doesn't like that kind of thing. He's not running a team like the Giants.

They have Chris Speier at shortstop and Tito Fuentes at second base. No matter what the situation, they play like they're ten games in front. They're always shouting at you, joking around, laughing, jockeying back and forth, and hot dogging like you wouldn't believe. It really bothers me.

I mean you slide into second trying to break up a double play and there they are, mouthing off and making fun of you and acting like they've got the world by the tail. That's not how Sparky wants his players acting.

So, when the game ends he shuts the doors and tells the guard not to let anybody in. He's got a few things on his mind, probably a lot of it left over from the frustration in San Diego, and he's going to let us know about it.

This is the first time Sparky's ever held a post-game meeting to chew us out and that's just what he does. He's seething, the veins sticking out in his neck and you knew he meant business.

211

"I've had enough of this," he says. "I'm tired of being a nice guy. Next year it's all gonna be different. I'm not going to be the same. I'm going back to the way I was and I'm going to see to it that things get done my way.

"I've created a monster, so it's up to me to destroy that monster and that's just what I'm going to do next year."

That's the gist of the meeting. He didn't like the attitude, giggling on errors, and he's right. I've got to give him credit. He saw something he didn't like and he spoke right up. But I'm not sure a meeting like that has any effect at all. We're just not the type of club to react to a chewing out. Especially not after winning an important game.

"He should have held the meeting in San Diego after we lost the first game," said Morgan. He was probably right. That was the time for it, but he was like the rest of us. He was down and couldn't believe we blew another chance to gain on the Dodgers. So, he kept it inside and a little laughing after an error triggered the explosion.

September 21
San Francisco

I couldn't believe my eyes. I stood there at the base of the left-field fence, looking up and saying over and over, "Son of a gun, son of a gun." It was the tenth inning of a baseball game we had to win and one we deserved to win.

We'd let the Giants score five runs in the first inning. Jack Billingham, the guy who has been our ace all year, was pitching. He was trying for his twentieth win. I can't quite understand what happened to Jack. It was the second time in a row he'd been bombed, this time getting only one man out. You can't let that happen. You have to reach back for something extra. You're going for a pennant and he's going for number 20. If that isn't enough incentive, I don't think you'll ever find enough.

212

But we fought back and tied in the ninth inning on a pinch-hit double by Terry Crowley. It was 6-6 and Pedro Borbon was pitching. Two were out and a man on when Ed Goodson, a left-handed hitter, slapped a line drive to left.

I got my butt back to the fence so the guy couldn't score from first. I couldn't believe it when that ball just kept going and going and cleared the wall for a two-run homer. All of a sudden it hit me. We'd lost.

I looked and Borbon was smashing his fist into his glove. I wanted to do the same thing but I couldn't. I was stunned. I mean you see an opposite field home run beat you maybe two, three times a year and it's usually by a McCovey or a Stargell. But Ed Goodson?

That homer right there killed us. The Dodgers won, 2-1, and they led by $3\frac{1}{2}$. More important, the magic number is seven and they are flying high while we're losing games to teams that shouldn't beat us.

The Giants are just going through the motions. It's cold out here and the crowds are small and the Giants don't want any part of playing. They're just putting in time. And they're killing us. To lose four out of six games to the Giants and the Padres—the two teams with the worst records in our division!

It just ain't meant to be this year.

September 22
San Francisco

This was the only fitting way for this road trip to come to an end, losing to a guy I hadn't heard of a week earlier. John Montefusco beat us, making it three out of four for the Giants and a 4-6 road trip. At just the time we needed our best trip of the year, we turn in our worst, and now all we can do is count off the days. The Dodgers' magic number is three and elimination is inevitable, unless you believe in miracles and, while I hold out hope, I know what's ahead.

John Montefusco has been dubbed "The Count" by his teammates, a pretty good nickname. You know, the Count of Montefusco. He's a right-hander and he throws from the side, which is the only way to throw in Candlestick Park. Out in left-center field there is this white sign, and a sidearmer's delivery comes right out of the sign. You can't see the ball.

I made sure Montefusco knew it, too. In the eighth inning I got to third and as he walked by, having backed up the base, I said to him, "We'll see if you pitch like this Friday night without a white sign in the background." He smiled. He knew the secret.

It was a helluva game for the kid. He pitched his first big league shutout. He hit a home run. He hustled on the bases and he made some good fielding plays. And he showed he's not awed by the big leagues.

For example, Griffey led off the third inning with a bunt single.

"Swing the bat," Montefusco yelled from the mound. That's being cocky, which is the way you're supposed to be. But I'm just not sure that angering major league veterans is the right thing to do. They remember.

Bench has a little remembering to do, too. In the fourth inning there were two out and Montefusco on first when Pat Darcy, another of the kids brought up from Indianapolis, threw a wild pitch. I guess Johnny thought the pitcher was on the bases so he didn't really go all out after the ball. Montefusco went from first to third and later said he did so because Bench didn't hustle. Johnny isn't going to like that.

There was something else Bench won't like. "Bench has always been my idol," Montefusco said after the game. "That's why I pitched harder to him than to anyone else." It showed. He struck Bench out three times.

214

And to think, Johnny thought it was funny when the kid walked up to the plate in the second inning and said, "Hi, Mr. Bench."

Two years ago John Montefusco was begging anyone for a tryout. He was playing semi-pro baseball and working for the telephone company as a complaints man. Now he's in the major leagues, beating the Cincinnati Reds and Don Gullett and, if that doesn't wrap up what's happened on this road trip, nothing will.

Oh, well, I'll be in the new house tomorrow and have everyone over for a party. It's easier to forget that way.

September 23
Cincinnati

It was housewarming time for the Pete Roses and what a house I have to warm. You'll have to excuse me if I brag about the new place a bit, but I'm a kid out of a neighborhood that isn't exactly the high rent district and now I've got nine rooms, four and a half baths, eight telephones, and five color television sets.

That's living. About $125,000 worth of living and I love every inch of it. We threw the party down in the game room, and just to give you an idea of what kind of party it was, we ran through nine fifths of scotch. There were about 60 people and the room's so big you'd have thought it was a party for four.

Some guys were shooting pool. Others were playing Ping-Pong. That's my specialty. I don't lose very often. Ray Knight, a rookie third baseman with us, thought he could play and I let him win a couple of games. Then I told him he wouldn't score ten points. He didn't.

He couldn't quite believe it. Over and over he kept mumbling, "You're just working on my head." I kept him running and all the time I'm talking to him . . . "Don't watch my eyes." . . . "You can't keep up with me, I'm a machine." . . . Hit this one." He didn't know where the ball was coming from.

I've got a room with all my plaques on the wall and I must admit I've got quite a few of them. I guess the MVP plaque is one of the nicer, but the one I cherish most is the Fred Hutchinson Award. That's named after our former manager and it's given to the man who best typifies his spirit and manhood. I like that award. He's the guy who gave me my break in the game and that's important to me.

There are the three silver bats there, too. They give those out for winning batting titles. The bats sit in a rack that was made by my father-in-law before he died. The first one is marked 1968 and the second 1969. The third is just marked 197?. He did that to give me something to shoot for, a third batting title, and I finally made it last year. I'm glad he got to see it because he was a helluva guy.

The house sort of symbolizes something else to me. I don't want to be traded. I just moved into the new house and in a couple of months I'm opening a restaurant in town. You know I want to stay around with those kind of things working.

As always, when a guy is 33 and has his batting average slip, they start talking about trading him. Tom Callahan, a columnist for the *Cincinnati Enquirer*, suggested it the other day. My wife almost went through the ceiling.

To be honest, I think deep down that I'll stay with the Reds. I know Sparky realizes what I mean to this club. But every once in a while, no matter who you are, you worry about it. It's part of the game and it does happen.

There was a quote from Sparky the other day that made me think. "If it was up to me, Pete Rose would never be traded from the Reds," the quote read.

That part about if it were up to Sparky is as if to say it isn't up to him and he might be outvoted by Bob Howsam. A guy like Howsam could trade me any time he wants. He's not from Cincinnati. He's an outsider.

I've been fortunate, not having to put up with being traded. But I know that it can happen, and if it does I hope it comes about before I'm too old to do a good job for my new team. And I want to wind up with a contender. I don't think I'm the type of player who could play on a team that wasn't a contender. What good is a winning attitude with a team that loses a hundred games a year?

I have the right to reject any trade I don't like. I know Howsam said a player wouldn't reject a trade just because he didn't want to go to a certain team. He believes no player would want to stay with a team that didn't want him.

That isn't so. There are some teams I wouldn't mind being traded to. The Yankees is one. I'd be in New York with a contender and playing for Gabe Paul, who used to run the Reds and whom I admire. I'd take the Mets or the Dodgers. And the Phils. I think I'd be a big hit with them, but my little buddy Larry Bowa would probably be mad. Instead of hitting second, he'd wind up hitting eighth.

Those are about the only teams I would go to and I mention them because they are about the only teams that could afford me. I wouldn't go just because I was traded, though. I'm like everyone else in this country. They'd have to offer me security and that would be a three-year contract. No one-year deal. What's to keep them from using me one year, then saying goodbye?

September 25
Cincinnati

When your lifetime average reads .312, as mine does, and

217

when you have .300 or more for nine straight years, as I have, you expect a bit of kidding when you go into the final days of the season with a .282 batting average, as I have.

So, I wasn't too surprised when the Houston Astros came to town and the talk was about Peter Edward Rose and his lack of hits.

"Hey, man," said Cliff Johnson, who is a big, strong backup catcher. "I read about you the other day. The story done said that Pete Rose still got the snap and the crackle but that he's lost the pop."

And my old buddy Tommy Helms couldn't wait to get on me. Even though he's almost a sure bet to be traded, he knows how to smile. What the hell, he's got one more year to run on his contract and he's hitting .281.

"How's it feel to be down there with the common folks?" he asked.

"Ah, c'mon. I ain't had a bad year. I just ain't had any luck," I said.

"You used your luck up the last ten years," he answered. "That's you, though, moaning over your luck. If you'd ever hit .237, like I did one year, you'd be crying."

"I can't hit .237," I answered.

"You said you couldn't hit .280," he said, and he's right. I really didn't think I could hit as low as .280. But I sure learned different this year.

I guess it was a long time ago that I realized I wouldn't get to .300 this year. I wanted to make it. It would have been something to have hit .300 for ten years in a row.

I keep looking back, trying to figure out what happened. Seems like every time I'd get going I'd run into a series where I'd go 3-for-7 and walk four times. I've walked more than a hundred times this year for the first time in my career and that hurt my average. If I'd been getting pitches to hit, I'd have gotten the hits I needed. I'm going to finish with about

185 hits, and without the walks I would have gone over 200 hits, which is one of my goals.

It always seemed to go wrong just when it seemed like it was going right. I'd have a good day, a 3-for-4, and sure enough I'd be 0-for-2, the next day with a couple of walks. I watched that happen time and again and I knew I wasn't going to get to .300.

Today I went to a Rotary Club meeting and a guy asked me what it feels like not to hit .300. Hell, I don't know. The last time I didn't hit .300 I was a kid. I just don't know the feeling yet.

But don't tell me I had a bad year. I know better than anyone that my average is down, but I just can't see how anyone can say I had a bad year. I've scored 100 runs. I lead the league in doubles. I have 100 walks. I've been on base as much as last year, scored almost as many runs, and gotten more extra base hits.

True, I'm not having the season I had in 1973, when I won the batting title, led the league in hitting, and had 230 hits. But in eleven years before I never had a year like that and I don't think I ever will again. If people expect me to have a year like 1973 every year, they'd better forget it. It's just impossible.

Whatever hopes we have we kept alive by beating Houston, 4-1, behind Clay Kirby and our rookie right-hander, Rawlins Jackson Eastwick III. I had a double, giving me a new career high of 43, hit a sacrifice fly, walked, and scored a run. One hit but not a bad night.

And how did the game end? With Cliff Johnson hitting a fly ball to the wall in center. And what did he yell at me as he headed back for the clubhouse?

"Hey, Pete. I got the snap and the crackle, but I've lost the pop, too."

I had to laugh.

219

David Concepcion takes a lot of kidding. The guys call him "Bozo." That comes from Bozo the Clown. Davey, you see, likes to wear outfits that are, to say the least, rather colorful.

Put him on a baseball field, though, and he's anything but a clown. He's merely the best shortstop in baseball, period. No one else combines his speed, power, range, and arm. He's almost the perfect athlete. He can jump far into the air and would have been a great basketball player. I've seen him on the court and he's got moves like Elgin Baylor or David Thompson. He took up golf this year and already is shooting in the 80's.

During the off-season in his native Venezuela he drives a Volkswagen in races and won his second race. He can do just about everything.

Tonight, he did it all as we beat the Giants, 4-3, to keep alive whatever hopes we have. And they are slim. Five games remain and we have to win them all.

In the seventh inning Davey reached one of the goals he's been shooting for. He became, as he put it, "El Babe Ruth de Venezuela." He hit his thirteenth homer of the season and no player from Venezuela ever hit so many home runs.

We have almost a monopoly on the South of the Border records. Tony Perez has hit more home runs than any other player from Cuba, and from the looks of things, that's a record that may stand forever, since there aren't any players coming out of Cuba.

"You hold the records in Cuba, roomie," Concepcion said to Perez, applying a delicate needle. "Home runs, runs batted in . . . strike-outs.

"I want to be king in Venezuela," Davey went on. "I want to hold all the records for my country."

220

Next year he'll probably add another. Luis Aparacio stole 58 bases in a season. Davey should break that easily. He's been thrown out only twice this year by a catcher, stealing 49.

He's the best Venezuelan export since oil.

"The Count" got his comeuppance tonight, just as I thought he would. You remember John Montefusco, the sidearming rookie right-hander who shut us out in San Francisco when he was throwing out of the white sign in left-center.

He started tonight. Lasted two innings and gave up five runs, including homers to Morgan and Bench.

And guess what? Griffey tried to bunt on him again.

"Swing the damn bat," shouted Montefusco.

"Throw the ball over and kiss my tail," countered Griffey.

Later, Griffey was still hot about Montefusco's attitude. "Next time, if there is a next time, I might just bunt down the first-base line and run up his back."

I believe Griffey will try it. He, after all, has to make a living from his legs and a big part of his game is bunting. If Montefusco wants to try to take that away from him, well, he has to be taught a lesson . . . even more of a lesson than he got today as we won 13-6 to keep the Dodgers from drinking champagne.

The magic number is one, and that means we've got to win the rest of our games while the Dodgers lose three in a row in Houston. I know that's not going to happen, but if you'd have been sitting in the Cincinnati clubhouse you'd have thought that I was alone in my belief. The talk was of miracles.

"If we win out something will happen," said Sparky, the eternal optimist. "I just have that feeling."

"I believe in miracles," added Concepcion. "It has happened before."

"Oh yeah? When?" I asked.

"With my ankle. I think I never play again and a lot of people think the same thing. But now I play."

But miracles? All this is going to do is keep me up all night again waiting for a Dodger score. Damn, I hope we keep winning so they don't drink champagne on us.

September 29
Cincinnati

The last home game of the year was played today and I spent more time on my belly than I did on my feet. In the third inning I doubled to left and slid head first into second base. In the sixth inning I walked, took second on a passed ball and third on a wild pitch, again going in head first. And in the eighth I tripled in a run, finishing off with a long, head-first dive into third.

I guess if anything has become the trademark of Charlie Hustle it has been the head-first slide.

I guess, too, if I'm asked a million questions, half of them are, "Why do you slide head first?" The answer to that is I slide head first because it's the only way to slide. When you slide that way you don't lose any momentum. In fact, you probably gain speed, and how many plays have you seen that were decided by an inch or so?

Another factor is that you can see what's going on. You know where the throw is and whether the fielder has caught the ball.

I like to think, too, that sliding head first is exciting. I know the fans like it and I think it helps inspire the guys on the team, too.

And, you don't take much of a beating. You skin up your forearms on occasion and sometimes a knee, but your belly doesn't take any punishment because you land on your forearms and skid right in.

Performing as I did today gave me a big kick, especially since 50,342 crowded their way into Riverfront Stadium. It was Fan Appreciation Day and our attendance wound up at 2,164,307. That kind of support deserves a winner and some day we're going to give it to them here.

October 1
Atlanta

The Dodgers managed somehow to lose again. We're still alive. We've got two games with the Braves and they have two with Houston.

Today the newspapers were full of something other than the pennant race, hard as that may be to believe. Frank Robinson is going to be named manager of the Cleveland Indians—the first black manager—and Gaylord Perry says he'll quit.

I guess not many people remember it, but the Robinson-Perry feud goes back to the days when Frank was a Red. It was 1965 in San Francisco. The bases were loaded, and Perry hit Robby with a pitch.

I guess Frank thought by the expression on Perry's face or by the way he threw the ball that it was done deliberately. Frank was the type of guy who, if he thought you were throwing at him, would let you know about it. That's what he did. They didn't quite get into it, but almost.

It was a battle between them that had been brewing for a long time and I guess neither of them ever got over it. But

223

now Frank's going to be the manager and Gaylord his star pitcher, and Perry had better come around. It wasn't Frank's fault that Bob Aspromonte was fired as manager of the Indians. If Frank and Gaylord don't get along, I don't see how Frank can succeed in Cleveland.

Robby has a chance to be a good manager. He definitely knows baseball and he has enough respect to be a manager. But it goes back to the same old thing: if a manager doesn't have the players, it doesn't matter how much baseball he knows. The fact that he has hit 600 home runs and is sure to be in the Hall of Fame doesn't insure that he's going to be a successful manager.

When Robby played with the Reds, he couldn't have managed. But he's learned a lot since then. He's learned how to win, and more important, how to lose. He's been with a good club—Baltimore—and a not-so-good club—California.

Robby keeps hearing the rap that he can't manage himself, so how is he going to manage 25 big league players. A lot of that talk goes back to the gun incident in Cincinnati. Well, let me tell you, that was blown out of proportion. He had a gun in his glove compartment. Often ballplayers have a tendency to carry a lot of money around. They like to have some protection, not that they'd ever use it.

Robby got a bum rap there. I think he's ready to manage and I wish him the best of luck. Maybe next year I can see him again . . . in the World Series.

October 2
Atlanta

There will be no World Series in Cincinnati this year. The Reds are dead. The Dodgers are the National League Western Division champions.

Buzz Capra and the Atlanta Braves beat us, eliminating

us from the race. Just to rub dirt in the wound, the Dodgers also won in Houston. It's over.

Jack Billingham went for his twentieth win again and got bombed. He managed to get only one man out, giving up three runs, and it was over.

I felt for Jack. I know how badly he wanted to win twenty and he pitched some great, clutch pressure games for us during the season. But when he had to have it, in his final four starts, he couldn't do it.

"What can I say?" he asked. "I just haven't done it when we needed it."

How right he was.

The feeling? Not as bad as you might think. I never did think the Dodgers would lose three in a row in Houston. But still, the inevitable hurts. When you believe you have the best team, you always think something's going to happen. It never did. We finished second.

And weird is the only way to describe the game that eliminated us. In the seventh inning we were still alive, down just 4-1, and Vic Correll led off for Atlanta. He hit what seemed to be a routine fly to Griffey in right. All of a sudden the ball went crazy and Griffey ducked out of the way. I couldn't believe what I was seeing.

The cover had come off the damn baseball. The stitching actually broke and the ball went crazy as it came at Griffey.

"It looked like a helicopter coming down at me," he told me later. "Scared hell out of me."

So it was over. I went to Morgan in the quiet dressing room.

"How do you feel?" I asked.

"I just don't know yet," he whispered. "I probably won't know until I'm watching the playoffs on television. Then it might be worse than I expect.

"I know I took it for granted this spring that we'd win. I

just knew we would. Maybe that was wrong. But I'll tell you something, Pete. Something like this makes me appreciate all the more the World Series I did get into. You just can't take anything for granted."

Henry Aaron ended the 1974 baseball season just as he started it tonight. On the final swing of his bat he hit home run number 733. In Riverfront Stadium, opening day, he hit number 714 to tie Babe Ruth on his first swing of the bat. He's unbelievable. So climactic. And what a guy.

The talk now is that Henry Aaron will not quit. I spoke to him and, while he wouldn't say for sure, I don't think he's going to call it a career. I hope not.

There are two reasons I hope Henry Aaron keeps playing. First, I still think he swings the bat as well as anyone. Second, he's great for baseball.

The word is that he's going to play for the Milwaukee Brewers in the American League, going back to the town in which he started 21 years ago. That would really help the American League. They need Henry Aaron. Baseball needs him. He's the most obliging superstar I've ever seen. You need an autograph, a bat, a ball, anything, he's got it for you. I've never heard another player say a bad word about him.

You just don't like to see him out of baseball. You don't like to see Willie Mays gone. And when Roberto Clemente died it was more than just a great player dying. Baseball lost a great asset. When a sport loses someone in that category, it's got to hurt the sport. Guys like Aaron, Mays, Clemente . . . they just aren't replaced.

Opening day seems so far away now. That was such a happy day—Aaron's homer and me scoring from second on a wild pitch to win, 8-7. And now 1974 is over. We were beaten, 13-0, by Phil Niekro, who won his twentieth. A long winter to rest. A winter to stop and think.

Then, it will be opening day again and this time it will be the Dodgers in Cincinnati. Next year should be a good year for me and the Reds. Every time I hit I will be setting a new record. I will pass 2,500 career hits on my way to 3,000, which is my goal.

And I have something to prove to the Dodgers. It seems as though my whole season was wrapped around them. They edged us for the pennant. The fans worked me over there but good. And I went 3-for-39 in Dodger Stadium. Take that away and I have my tenth straight .300 season.

Oh, well, it couldn't go on forever. Not even for Charlie Hustle.

October 4
Cincinnati

This is always a sad day—the day after the season ends and you are cleaning out your locker, looking at the souvenirs of a season and knowing that someone else is playing in the playoffs and World Series.

I was throwing all the stuff in a bag with little Petie helping me. Sparky came up.

"I want to be traded to Los Angeles," said Petie.